ENERGY EFFICIENCY POLICIES

D1634519

It is generally assumed, in economics and politics, that the atmosphere is 'free'. However, the greenhouse effect and global warming have shown this to be a false assumption and the need for active policies to promote preservation of this finite resource are becoming ever more urgent.

In *Energy Efficiency Policies*, Victor Anderson argues for alternative policies to promote energy efficiency in response to the changing composition of the atmosphere and global warming. As the industrialised West consumes half the world's energy, despite accounting for only one-sixth of the global population, the study focuses on energy policies in the OECD. The argument centres on the need to end the greenhouse effect by making the transition from a carbon economy to one based on renewable resources. This in turn raises the case for the introduction of the controversial Progressive Carbon Tax. However, energy efficiency policies may, at least in the short term, be expensive to implement. The author illustrates some of these economic difficulties by use of case-studies, including the government's attempts to promote energy efficiency in the UK and the least cost approach adopted in the USA. Victor Anderson concludes with a summary of 15 possible efficiency policies. In an area that is generally dominated by highly specialised literature, *Energy Efficiency Policies* is accessible and offers a practical and topical guide to tackling the effects of global warming and preserving the earth's atmosphere.

Victor Anderson is a researcher for the New Economics Foundation, a charitable organisation which grew out of *The Other Economic Summit* (*TOES*) whose aims are to promote 'a New Economics which is humane, just, sustainable and based on people's needs'. His publications include *Alternative Economic Indicators* (1991).

ENERGY EFFICIENCY POLICIES

Victor Anderson

London and New York

First published 1993
by Routledge
11 New Fetter Lane, London EC4P 4EE

Simultaneously published in the USA and Canada
by Routledge
29 West 35th Street, New York, NY 10001

© 1993 New Economics Foundation

Typeset in Garamond by Witwell Ltd, Southport
Printed and bound in Great Britain by
Mackays of Chatham PLC, Chatham, Kent

British Library Cataloguing in Publication Data

A catalogue record for this book is available from the British Library

ISBN 0-415-08696-5 cased
0-415-08697-3 Pbk

Library of Congress Cataloging-in-Publication Data
has been applied for

CONTENTS

ACKNOWLEDGEMENTS

I would like to thank British Petroleum and British Telecom for the financial support which has enabled me to write this book. The report was supported by BT as part of its community programme.

I would also like to thank the following people for their comments, help, and advice: Trevor Blackwell, Hazel Cadenhead, John Chesshire, Tim Crabtree, John Davis (who suggested to me the idea of a 'Progressive Carbon Tax'), Paul Ekins, Dieneke Ferguson, Mike Flood, Tim Jackson, Michael Jacobs, Alan Jarvis, George McRobie, Ed Mayo, Aubrey Meyer, Joan Rawlinson, Andy Roberts, James Robertson, Danyal Sattar, Diana Schumacher, and Perry Walker.

Victor Anderson,
New Economics Foundation,
London

INTRODUCTION

Conventional economics has ignored the fact that the atmosphere is a basic resource, essential to life and livelihoods. Economic theory has generally followed the price system in treating the atmosphere as 'free', and hence has failed to see that its capacities are finite, and on their way to becoming scarce. New Economics is challenging this outlook, reconceptualising the economic process so that manufacturing industry and other parts of the formal money economy are seen as dependent on a base of unpaid domestic activity, and an even more fundamental base of 'nature's economy': the biosphere, geology, and atmosphere of the planet.[1]

The aim of this book is to apply the New Economics approach to the issue of government policies to promote energy efficiency in response to the changing composition of the atmosphere and the rising threat of global warming. The focus of the book is on the industrialised West (defined here as the member countries of the OECD: the Organisation for Economic Co-operation and Development).

The reason for choosing to focus on the industrialised West is that we consume half the world's energy, despite being only one-sixth of the world's people. Energy consumption per person is therefore five times as high within the OECD as the average in the rest of the world. If there is a problem for the world about energy consumption – and there is – then it is primarily a problem about economics and lifestyles in the OECD West.[2]

Global warming has virtually every imaginable problematic feature that an environmental issue can have. The scale and speed of global warming itself are uncertain; its social and economic impacts are uncertain; the phenomenon is complex, with many different causes, effects, and feedback mechanisms; many of the solutions proposed are contrary to what most people see as their own self-interest, and hence either what they are prepared to do voluntarily or to vote for; there is a time-lag between causes and effects so that by the time the evidence becomes literally impossible to ignore it is too late to do anything effective about it; no existing political authority has the competence or sovereignty to properly deal with the issue because it is global in scale; and if we fail to solve the problem, the risks involved are enormous.

Energy efficiency is crucial for global warming because it can make a major impact on carbon dioxide emissions fairly quickly and fairly cheaply (perhaps even saving money in the process). In this book, I shall discuss energy use rather than energy supply – though in the long term there also needs to be increased efficiency in energy supply and a shift away from fossil fuels towards solar and other renewable sources of energy.

The technology already exists to make Western economies far more efficient in their energy use, but unfortunately the ways in which economies are organised at present operates to discourage the use of this technology. The economics of energy efficiency needs to be changed, and government action is essential in order to achieve this.

OUTLINE OF THE BOOK

Chapter 1 is about the carbon cycle and the greenhouse effect itself, and about the need to make a transition from the 'Carbon Economy' of the present to an economy based on renewable sources of energy.

Chapter 2 presents the case for introducing a Carbon Tax, and the problems which this raises. Most of the rest of the book is about these problems and the task of devising policies which can respond to them.

Chapter 3 looks at energy efficiency and the arguments which have been put forward for promoting it. It also includes statistics on trends in energy use. Chapter 4 is about the causes of energy inefficiency, showing that many of the barriers to efficiency in energy use cannot be dealt with by Carbon Tax on its own.

Chapter 5 outlines the various types of policies which governments in OECD countries have implemented up to now in order to promote energy efficiency. Chapter 6 is a short history of energy efficiency policies in the UK over the past 20 years. Chapter 7 looks at 'least cost planning' and at US policies which have promoted energy efficiency through this approach.

Chapter 8 draws some conclusions and recommends fifteen policies for combating global warming and promoting energy efficiency, including a 'Progressive Carbon Tax' (PCT).

There are also three appendices. Appendix 1 is a critique of the application of cost–benefit analysis to the problem of global warming. Appendix 2 is about the New Economics Foundation which works on, and promotes debate about, the application of green and humanistic approaches to economic issues: 'economics as if people and the planet mattered'. Appendix 3 is a short bibliography of books taking a broadly 'New Economics' approach.

1

THE CARBON CRISIS

Carbon, the basis of life, is becoming a threat to life. Whilst it makes sense to talk about a general 'ecological crisis', there is also a specific crisis of humanity's relationship to one element in particular: carbon.

Alarm bells don't automatically ring in our heads at the mention of the word 'carbon'. It isn't inherently toxic, the planet copes with large quantities of it already, and it is so essential to life that it is contained in the bodies of every living organism. Scientists refer to 'the carbon cycle', representing the various ways in which carbon atoms flow through plants, animals, and the physical environment.

What has pushed the carbon cycle into a state of crisis is, above all, the very large-scale use of fossil fuels by industrial economies, increasing the amount of carbon dioxide in the atmosphere and causing global warming. Industrial economies are taking carbon-based fossil fuels and transforming them from resources into pollutants. There are other elements of the crisis too: methane, which also contains carbon, contributes to global warming, as does the destruction of tropical rainforests which are at present massive stores of carbon.

Carbon has become the basis for life because of its exceptionally strong ability to link atoms together. Carbon-based fossil fuels are the source of most of our energy supplies because energy is derived from breaking those atoms apart. Once broken, they turn into waste, now accumulating in increasingly dangerous quantities.

This chapter looks at how the natural carbon cycle operates, how human industrial activity has affected this cycle, what results this is having, and what types of solutions are possible. The next chapter will discuss the contribution which economics and the workings of the economy have made, and are still making, to the carbon crisis, and

1

what sort of economics and economic policy would be part of a solution.

THE CARBON CYCLE.

The 'carbon cycle' is the ways in which carbon flows through the living and non-living world. At any one time, some carbon is in the atmosphere, some in water, some in soil, some in rock, and some in the bodies of living organisms, including human beings. The movement of carbon atoms from one location to another is one of the main ways in which the different parts of the planet are connected. The carbon cycle is a vast process of recycling, storing, and reusing carbon.

One part of the carbon cycle takes place on land and involves photosynthesis. Plants take in water, and carbon dioxide from the air, and with the aid of energy provided by sunlight, turn them into a combination of oxygen, which goes back to the air, and carbohydrates which become part of the plants themselves. Animals which eat the plants use the energy stored up in the carbohydrates to provide energy for their own bodies, for movement, keeping warm, etc. Almost all living things depend on photosynthesis, either directly or indirectly. Photosynthesis, and the consumption of its products (e.g. by animals eating plants), is, amongst other things, a flow of carbon.

When plants and animals die and decay some carbon enters the atmosphere and some goes into the soil. Some of what goes into the soil eventually turns into peat, coal, oil, and natural gas. The fossil fuels we use today are the result of photosynthesis millions of years ago.

Another part of the carbon cycle involves the exchange of carbon beween the atmosphere and the oceans. Roughly half of all carbon dioxide produced dissolves in the oceans, some of it combining with calcium to become calcium carbonate (limestone), and some entering the food chain by being absorbed by plankton, which is then eaten by fish and other sea creatures.

The quantities of carbon involved in all these processes are enormous, and those which are released by human activity, such as the burning of fossil fuels and deforestation, are small by comparison. The problem is that the natural carbon cycle is in balance: the amount of carbon that leaves the atmosphere each year is equal to the amount that joins it. Although a lot of carbon passes through the atmosphere there is no net build-up over the years, though there are seasonal fluctuations as carbon is embodied in plants during the spring and summer and returns to the atmosphere in the autumn.

Human activity in the industrial era has added more and more extra carbon dioxide. The current proportion of carbon dioxide in the atmosphere is estimated to be 25 per cent above pre-industrial levels. Methane, which combines carbon with hydrogen, has more than doubled.

THE RISE OF THE CARBON ECONOMY

Modern industrial economies are based on two massive sources of subsidy: cheap raw materials and labour from 'third world' countries, and carbon-based fossil fuels. In using the fossil fuels of coal, oil, and natural gas, we are using the stored energy of past photosynthesis: the carbon dioxide, water, and sunlight of millions of years ago. Industrial economies are currently using it up at a speed which is in the order of a million times faster than the rate at which fossil fuels were originally accumulated.

The enormous energy of fossil fuels created and drove the Industrial Revolution. Complex machinery and instruments existed long before then, but what was lacking was a source of energy which could add power to machines on a large scale. The key to early industrialisation was the use of coal in steam engines, used to drive the railways and textile and other manufacturing machinery. This was followed in the second half of the nineteenth century by the widespread use of petroleum. In the twentieth century, coal and petroleum have both been used in power stations to generate electricity.

In all of these ways, human beings have taken the products of the natural carbon cycle, used them in economic activities, and created as one of the results a build-up of carbon-based gases in the atmosphere. Until recently this has seemed to be a very small price to pay for the huge expansion in production and prosperity which 'the Carbon Economy' has brought about. But now the negative consequences loom much larger than they used to.

EFFECTS ON THE CARBON CYCLE

The three most important parts of the current carbon crisis are the build-up of carbon dioxide, the build-up of methane, and the destruction of tropical rainforests. All three contribute to the greenhouse effect, which is causing global warming. All three prevent the carbon cycle from being in balance.

Carbon dioxide and methane in the atmosphere trap energy from the Sun, stopping some of it from radiating out again into space. This is useful because warmth is retained for plant, animal, and human use. Pre-industrial levels of carbon dioxide and methane were sufficient to secure this. Current levels of these gases, however, are more than enough, and are resulting in the planet gradually heating up. Although it is impossible to predict all the consequences of the greenhouse effect, the most obvious general outcome is a rise in sea-level. Many coastal areas will be completely flooded and others will be increasingly invaded by saltwater, making agriculture less and less feasible. The general temperature rise itself – together with the changes in wind and rainfall it is already starting to produce – is causing further problems for agriculture, including crop failures and droughts in some regions. Heating up the oceans causes evaporation from them to increase, creating more and worse hurricanes and cyclones. Flooding and changes in climate are also likely to extend the regions affected by insect-borne and water-borne diseases. The rate of species extinctions will increase because many plants and animals will be unable to adapt to the new conditions at the speed which will be necessary if they are to survive. Overall, the impact of the greenhouse effect will be disastrous.[1]

Carbon dioxide is estimated to account for about 55 per cent of the combined impact of all the gases which contribute to the greenhouse effect; 15 per cent is accounted for by methane, 24 per cent by CFCs and halons, and 6 per cent by nitrous oxide, together with an additional unquantifiable contribution from tropospheric ozone (ozone much nearer to the surface of the Earth than the ozone layer is).[2] Depletion of the ozone layer by CFCs (chlorofluorocarbons) and halons also contributes to global warming because it results in increases in the amount of solar radiation reaching the Earth's surface.

The burning of fossil fuels – directly, and in electricity generation – is estimated to produce about 70 per cent or 80 per cent of carbon dioxide emissions. Fossil fuels also contribute to emissions of methane (mainly by natural gas leaks) and nitrous oxide, and to the build-up of tropospheric ozone. Increasing concentrations of methane are also caused by agriculture, especially by rice growing and cattle, and from burning wood as a fuel.

In addition, deforestation destroys a means by which carbon is stored, and where forest trees are burned, further carbon dioxide is added to the atmosphere. Deforestation also has some 'non-carbon crisis' effects, including disruption of the cycle by which water circulates through the environment, and destruction of plant and animal habitats, adding to species extinctions.

Every substance becomes toxic if it is at a high enough level of concentration. This is now starting to happen with carbon in the atmosphere in the form of both carbon dioxide and methane, amounting together to more than two-thirds of the greenhouse effect. With some substances, the solutions are simple because they represent a relatively minor part of existing economies and ways of life. This is true of the ozone-destroying CFCs, for example. But carbon is not like that. It is the key to modern economies.

ACID POLLUTION

As well as the problems which current large-scale use of fossil fuels cause for the carbon cycle, they also contribute to overproduction of acidic sulphur and nitrogen oxides, much of it in the form of acid rain. This acid pollution affects air, soil, lakes, and rivers, and results in damage to trees and other plant life, fish, buildings, and human health. It is caused mainly by sulphur dioxide reacting with other substances to create sulphuric acid, and nitrogen oxides reacting to form nitric acid. Sulphur dioxide and nitrogen oxides are created mainly by the burning of carbon-based fossil fuels.

Although there are other ways of reducing sulphur dioxide and nitrogen oxides emissions – such as the use of low-sulphur coal, the removal of sulphur from the gases given off by coal-burning, and catalytic converters to reduce nitrogen oxides emissions from cars – the most straightforward and effective way of combating acid pollution is simply through the reduction of fossil fuel use.

An important feature of the economics of acid pollution is that there is often a considerable distance between cause and effect: a fossil fuel burned in Britain may cause pollution in Scandinavia; the USA causes acid rain in Canada; China causes problems for Japan, etc., depending primarily on which way the winds blow. Successful policies will require international bargaining, and perhaps compensation of some form.[3]

THE NUCLEAR ECONOMY

There are basically two ways out of the carbon crisis, both involving switching away from fossil fuels to more use of other sources of energy. One way is to move from the carbon economy to the nuclear economy, based on plutonium and uranium. The other way is to move to what I shall call 'the renewable economy', based on solar, wind, and wave power, and also including greater energy efficiency and new economic rules to limit the use of the atmosphere. Before discussing ideas about a renewable economy, it is important first to look at the nuclear option.

Very large increases in the amount of energy generated by nuclear power would be necessary to make any significant impact on the greenhouse effect. This is because nuclear power at present provides only about 3 per cent of the total energy delivered to consumers worldwide. It has been estimated that existing nuclear power stations make carbon dioxide emissions just 4 per cent lower than they would be if fossil fuels were used in their place.[4] A very large programme of new investment in nuclear power would be necessary in order to produce reductions in emissions comparable to those which could be brought about by modest improvements in energy efficiency.[5]

A large-scale programme of investment in nuclear power would bring its own major risks and costs. We would be out of the greenhouse frying pan and into the nuclear fire. The environmental costs of nuclear power include:

1 Nuclear accidents. Accurate estimates of risk have been impossible to arrive at, but there is now a substantial history of nuclear power in practice. This includes the incidents at Three Mile Island in 1979 and Chernobyl in 1986, and, on a smaller scale, the fire at Windscale in 1957 and numerous other accidents, mainly attributed to 'human error'.

2 Radioactive waste. This is produced at all stages of the nuclear cycle, from uranium mining through to reprocessing. A great deal of low-level waste has already entered the general environment, increasing radiation levels, and the problem remains of how to store high-level wastes safely enough for long enough to prevent large-scale escapes of radioactivity.

3 Nuclear proliferation. Plutonium is used not only in nuclear power stations but also in nuclear bombs. The civil nuclear power industry developed out of nuclear weapons programmes in the USA, UK, USSR, and France. The civil and military uses of plutonium are

6

difficult to keep separate, and there are fears that many govern-ments are developing nuclear power partly to give themselves material for nuclear weapons, or at least the potential for generat-ing such material. There is also a possibility that plutonium might fall into the hands of non-government terrorist organisations.

THE RENEWABLE ECONOMY

The second way out of the carbon crisis is to move from the carbon economy, based on fossil fuels, over to a renewable economy, based on energy efficiency and renewable sources of energy.

The most basic point about a renewable economy is that it would be founded on a recognition that the economy is embedded in ecology. Natural resources derive from the environment, and waste products go back to the environment. If the workings of an economy threaten to go beyond the limits set by the natural world – as our use of carbon threatens to do – then that economy will not be sustainable. The way to make an economy sustainable is: (1) to recognise that it is essential to stay within the natural limits; (2) to try to discover as accurately and as early as possible what those limits are; and (3) to establish and maintain economic 'signals' such as prices, taxes, subsidies, and various forms of rationing and licensing, which enable the economy to respond appropriately to the best available estimates of the limits.

The economy and ecology are not equals. Although they are interdependent, the more fundamental dependence is the dependence of the economy on ecology. The biosphere existed long before the modern economy did, and long before any human beings. It is likely to exist in some form long after human beings disappear. Without the resources of the biosphere, geology, and atmosphere of the planet, there would be nothing to make an economy *from*. They can accurately be called the 'very long-term supply side' of the economy. No environment – no economy.

A 'renewable economy' would not necessarily have to be a no-growth economy in the sense that the Gross National Product couldn't rise, because GNP is a measure of monetary transactions in an economy, not a measure of its environmental impact.[6] But there would be various specific ways in which it would need to be a no-growth economy, including no growth in the consumption of carbon.

A renewable and no-carbon-growth economy would need to oper-ate much more like the natural world than the economy does at present. As the example of the carbon cycle demonstrates, in nature there are no wastes in the sense that all wastes are reused. The carbon atoms in dead animals and plants go round in the cycle and are used again in future animals and plants. Much of the rubbish and pollution which human beings have created through industrial processes, however, cannot be reused. It remains rubbish and pollution, continually accumulating, in some cases heading for critical levels.

A renewable economy would recycle and reuse resources much more than the existing economy does. In place of a throughput system with resources coming in at one end, and rubbish and pollution coming out the other, it would be a system of cycles in which resources circulated through the economy from one use to the next, in the same sort of way as carbon does in nature's economy.

This is an ideal picture, and in addition to numerous specific problems about how all this could be done, there is a major problem about energy, because energy cannot be recycled or reused in this way. Useful energy inevitably gets used up. The recycling and reuse of other resources would in many cases also save energy, but there would remain a problem about energy use. The two key principles for its use in a renewable economy would have to be: use renewable sources of energy, and use energy efficiently.

Renewable sources of energy are those which have a (virtually) permanent source, such as the Sun, wind, and the tides, and do not create waste on the scale of carbon fuels and nuclear power. The most important shift necessary in patterns of energy use is the shift from non-renewable to renewable sources of energy.

This will take quite a long time to achieve on a large scale. Given the urgency of the carbon crisis, other measures are also necessary in the short- and medium-term. Most of these should be based on the principle that wherever energy is used, especially if it is from non-renewable sources, it should be used efficiently. There is plenty of evidence that some existing technologies already make it possible to use energy far more efficiently than it is generally used at present. What is missing is the political and economic policies to unlock these technologies, so that they are used in practice on a much larger scale. Such policies are the main concern of this book.

2

THE PRICE OF AIR

THE TRIPLE SUBSIDY

Two different global systems coexist with difficulty on this planet. One is the global ecological system, which includes processes such as the carbon cycle. Human beings have added a second system, the global economic system. As with ecology, there is continuous interaction between the different parts of the system, in this case involving the buying and selling of commodities, shares, currencies, goods and services, around the world. Like the ecological system, this system also has its stresses and strains, but because it is a system set up and run by human beings (with the help of human-created technologies), these stresses and strains are generally far more familiar to us than the stresses and strains of the global ecological system. The carbon crisis is one part of a general problem about the relationship between these two global systems.

The fundamental problem underlying the carbon crisis is that the natural world – in this case, specifically the atmosphere – has been regarded as 'free', rather than as something extremely valuable. The use of the atmosphere, and its capacity to assimilate and recycle waste products, is 'free' in the straightforward financial sense that you don't have to pay for it. It is just treated as a 'given'. Unless there happen to be legal restrictions on pollution levels, or 'smokeless zones' limiting the burning of coal, the atmosphere can simply be used without limit.

What is wrong here is that the economy fails to register the fact that a resource (the capacities of the atmosphere) is being used up. Because the economy fails to register that fact, it fails to bring about a response to it – such as using the atmosphere more carefully, cautiously, efficiently. The present pattern of fossil fuel use shows that the 'free' atmosphere, together with the fossil fuels themselves,

9

have created a triple subsidy: subsidy in time, both from the past and the future, and subsidy in space.

The subsidy which modern industrial economies get from the past is the fossil fuels themselves. The subsidy we get from the future is that modern economies are using up the capacity of the atmosphere to deal with carbon. Future generations are subsidising present generations, in the sense that an equal sharing of the atmosphere would imply much less use of it now, leaving much more use possible in the future.

The subsidy in space derives from the fact that people in different parts of the world are using up the atmosphere at very different rates. Poorer people are subsidising richer people in the sense that an equal sharing of the atmosphere's capacity would imply much less use of it by the countries of the 'West' and much more use by the 'South'.

Present generations in the West are therefore gaining from a triple subsidy: subsidy from the past, subsidy from future generations, and subsidy from the 'Third World'. Modern 'advanced' economies owe their phenomenal production and wealth largely to this triple subsidy.

All three parts of the triple subsidy are threatening to desert us. The exhaustion of fossil fuel reserves – the subsidy from the past – is still a long way off, but some reserves are set to disappear much sooner. In the UK, the most important example is obviously North Sea oil, which will disappear early in the next century. The subsidy from future generations will be used up as the atmosphere's capacity becomes overloaded. The subsidy from the 'South' will also disappear as Southern countries increasingly industrialise and take their own share of what remains of the 'free' atmosphere.

The Western government which has gone furthest in acknowledging the existence of the triple subsidy is the government of The Netherlands. The Dutch *National Environmental Policy Plan* takes as one of its starting points the definition of 'sustainable development' used in *The Brundtland Report*: development that 'meets the needs of the present without compromising the ability of future generations to meet their own needs'.[1] It points out that present patterns of economic development, in contrast, *do* compromise the ability of future generations to meet their needs. The Dutch government sees this as part of a general problem about the economy and the environment:

> Environmental problems are . . . rolled off constantly to other people, other places and the future . . . This roll off leads to

sizeable 'environmental loans' on a worldwide scale. The current generation is consuming huge amounts of energy and other raw materials, leaving (chemical) waste belts behind everywhere, destroying fertile regions, chopping down unique rain forests, heating up the atmosphere, creating a hole in the ozone layer. All of this poses serious dangers to the pursuit of sustainable development.[2]

As part of a general approach of seeking to prevent this 'rolling off', the Dutch government have adopted the following principle: 'The general point of departure in funding measures to prevent and solve environmental problems is that the expense may not be passed on to future generations.'[3]

CARBON TAX

Basic economic theory suggests that if something is being used up at too fast a rate its price should be increased. In the case of the atmosphere, which is 'free', the crucial step is for it to have a price at all. The obvious solution to the carbon crisis is to charge for the use of the atmosphere, so that every time people use a carbon-based fossil fuel they have to pay twice: once for the fuel itself, and a second time for the pollution caused. The pollution charge could be included in the price of the fuel by means of taxation.

This reasoning has led to a variety of proposals being put forward based on the idea of a 'Carbon Tax'. The idea is that fuel should be taxed on the basis of the amount of carbon in it. The carbon content of a fuel, together with the quantity of fuel used, determines how much carbon dioxide will be released into the atmosphere.

Carbon-based fuels vary in their carbon content: coal would have to be taxed more heavily than oil, for example, and oil more heavily than gas. Non carbon-based fuels, such as nuclear power and the renewable sources of energy, would escape the tax and become relatively more economically attractive options.

The likely outcomes of Carbon Tax would be: (1) switching from one carbon-based fuel to another, e.g. from coal to gas, (2) switching from carbon-based fuels to non carbon-based fuels, e.g. from oil to nuclear or solar energy; (3) using fuels more efficiently to achieve the same result; (4) switching from fuel use to substitutes (e.g. from energy-intensive car journeys to phone calls) or to doing without. In all of these ways a Carbon Tax could be expected to bring about a reduction in carbon dioxide emissions.

Although this argument for Carbon Tax appears to be basically valid, naturally the reality is far more complex than the previous few paragraphs imply. This book is concerned with identifying the significant complexities involved, and with the effort to devise a set of policies – a context of *additional measures* to complement Carbon Tax, and a *particular version* of Carbon Tax – which take into account these complexities. There are four major problems about Carbon Tax itself: non-price influences (which the tax will fail to deal with), distributional impact, elasticity, and macroeconomic impact.

The problem of non-price influences

One of the factors which prevents Carbon Tax by itself from being able to deal adequately with the carbon crisis is 'non-price' influences on the use of fossil fuels. In other words, fossil fuels are used on the current scale not simply because they are relatively cheap, but also because of influences other than their price. If the price of fuel doubled, for example, its use would not necessarily immediately fall: a number of other changes might have to take place first, such as an expansion in public transport to make it practical for less people to drive to work, and time to find out about how to use energy more efficiently and put the more energy-efficient methods and technologies in place.

Chapter 4 will outline a variety of influences other than price which limit the efficiency with which energy is currently used. Since one of the main objectives of Carbon Tax is increased energy efficiency, these non-price reasons for inefficiency will need to be tackled by devising appropriate policies to be implemented alongside Carbon Tax.

The problem of distributional impact

In any country which operates any tax, there is a 'distributional impact'. Taxes vary as to which sections of the population they have the greatest impact on. In the case of a UK Carbon Tax, the greatest impact is likely to be on poorer people, effectively making them still poorer. In addition to the problem this creates about social justice and equity, this regressive distributional impact also influences the political acceptability of Carbon Tax proposals, i.e. whether people are prepared to vote for parties which advocate Carbon Tax, and whether parties are prepared to run any electoral risks involved in advocating it. The distributional impact is obviously a particular barrier in Britain to getting Labour Party and 'poverty lobby' support for Carbon Tax.

A study of the distributional impact of a UK Carbon Tax was carried out in 1990 at the Institute for Fiscal Studies (IFS).[4] The IFS authors show (using figures from the 1986 *Family Expenditure Survey*) that the average expenditure on domestic fuel of the richest 10 per cent of households was just over *twice* that of the poorest 10 per cent of households (£16.92 compared to £7.95). But since the average total expenditure of the top 10 per cent was *more than eight* times that of the bottom 10 per cent, and their average income was about *sixteen* times as great, domestic fuel expenditure took up a much lower proportion of richer people's incomes and spending than it did of poorer people's incomes and spending.[5] The study concluded that a tax on domestic fuel (which is currently zero-rated for VAT purposes) would therefore have much less impact on richer people than on poorer people.

The overall effect of taxing domestic fuel – whether through a Carbon Tax or bringing domestic fuel within the scope of Value Added Tax – would be likely to be little change in fuel consumption by richer people, a significant fall in fuel consumption by poorer people, and a fall in the purchasing power of poorer people.

> The distributional effects of the change are strongly adverse. The increase in tax paid by households in the lowest decile [10 per cent] by income would be £1 a week [assuming 15 per cent VAT on domestic fuel], and that of the richest 10 per cent of households would be around £2, yet the richest decile are sixteen times richer before tax than the poorest. Worse still, the poorest decile cut their consumption of energy by 10 per cent, whereas the richest decile would hardly reduce their consumption at all.[6]

The projected cut in consumption is 9.9 per cent for the poorest, but only 1.2 per cent for the richest.

Since it is the richest who are consuming most energy and emitting most carbon dioxide, and the poorest who are most likely to suffer from problems with cold and damp housing, this seems neither a fair nor an effective way of dealing with the issue. The impact would obviously be still greater if moves were made beyond 15 per cent to the far higher tax rates proposed by many advocates of a Carbon Tax.

The problem of distributional impact is a key problem to take into account, both in devising a set of policies to go along with Carbon Tax, and in devising a particular version of the tax. It does not, however, necessarily imply abandoning the whole idea of a Carbon Tax, provided the problem can in fact be dealt with through additions and modifications. This issue will be discussed further in Chapter 8, where a Progressive Carbon Tax is advocated.

The problem of elasticity

In devising a Carbon Tax, a key question obviously is: how much should it be? This depends on two things: how much do carbon emissions need to be constrained by (which in turn depends on the impact of carbon emissions on the greenhouse effect and the impact of the greenhouse effect itself), and what rate of tax is necessary in order to constrain emissions by that amount?

Different rates of tax imply different percentage changes in the prices of particular fuels. A well-established instrument of economic analysis is the 'price elasticity of demand', which is a measure of the sensitivity of consumers to changes in price. In order to find out what price changes will be necessary to bring about a particular reduction in the use of carbon-based fuels we need to know what the price elasticity of demand for those fuels is.

This is not a simple matter, for a number of reasons. Firstly, price elasticity of demand varies with time-period. If someone only has a short period in which to react to a price rise, they may simply carry on with the same behaviour, just putting up with the rise in price. Time is needed for behaviour to change and for new, more energy-efficient, domestic appliances to be purchased, for example. Rises in fuel prices which look after one year as if they have had little effect on demand may turn out after five years to have had an enormous effect. Price elasticity of demand must be judged over a realistic time-period.

Secondly, the prices of products affect demand not only for those products, but also for products which are substitutes for them. For example, if butter becomes more expensive, that not only reduces demand for butter but also increases the demand for margarine, even if margarine prices are unchanged. This is the 'cross-elasticity of demand'. Carbon Tax proposals involve a number of elasticities and cross-elasticities simultaneously: a rise in coal prices will affect demand for oil and gas, a rise in oil prices will affect demand for gas and coal, and a rise in gas prices will affect demand for coal and oil.

Thirdly, a lot depends on what is, and what becomes, technologically possible. A high rate of Carbon Tax may be an incentive to a firm to switch to a different method of production, but a different method may not yet exist at the time the tax is first imposed. Forecasting the effect of the tax depends on being able to forecast whether or not the technological development will take place which will enable the firm to actually switch to a different method of production. Changes in demand on the basis of existing technological options are a poor guide to the longer-term shifts which may take place as a result of the tax combined with future technological change.

A further complication is that the tax will itself affect the pre-tax price as suppliers accept some drop in their profit margins in preference to a fall in their sales. The percentage rate of tax doesn't therefore neatly translate into an equal percentage rate of price increase. If profit margins are squeezed, the resulting price increase will be less than the tax rate.

Various economists have attempted to arrive at estimates for the rate of Carbon Tax which would be necessary in order to bring about an adequate degree of restraint in carbon dioxide emissions. Because of all the uncertainties involved, there is a wide variation between different estimates of the tax rates required.[7]

The problem of macroeconomic impact

Once the rate of Carbon Tax has been selected, a further set of issues arises about the impact which a given rate of tax will have on the economy as a whole. A rate of Carbon Tax high enough to do something effective about carbon emissions might conceivably also wreck the economy of the country introducing it.

The macroeconomic impact of Carbon Tax depends crucially on three factors. The first is obviously the rate of Carbon Tax itself: a small tax is likely to have only a small impact on macroeconomic variables like inflation and unemployment. The second factor is what happens to the revenue raised from Carbon Tax. If it is taken out of the economy, either by being saved by government (or used to repay government debt), or by being handed over to an international authority which saves it or spends it in another country, then the level of demand will fall by the amount of the revenue collected in Carbon Tax. If it is spent by government within the country, then the level of total demand should be unchanged by the tax, and so again the impact on variables such as inflation and unemployment should be relatively small. The third factor is the impact of the tax on competitiveness in international trade: this depends primarily on whether the tax is levied on imports, and on whether competitor countries are also introducing the tax themselves (perhaps as a result of international agreement).

After reviewing various recent studies of the macroeconomic impact of Carbon Tax, Dr Michael Grubb, in *Energy Policies and the Greenhouse Effect*, concluded: 'most studies . . . suggest that even high levels would have only a small impact on growth, assuming the revenues from the tax to be recycled domestically'.[8] It is worth pointing out also that the macroeconomic impact of not having a Carbon Tax, and not acting effectively against the greenhouse effect, is likely to be extremely large in the long term.[9]

16

3

ARGUMENTS AND TRENDS

The current debate about energy efficiency focuses mainly on the problem of carbon emissions and global warming, but many of the policies which have been suggested as means of promoting energy efficiency derived originally from quite different rationales. In order to analyse the variety of policy ideas it is useful to examine the range of different arguments which have been put forward by those advocating them.

It is possible to distinguish between five different types of reason for advocating energy efficiency. There is no inherent conflict between them: it would be perfectly possible for someone to rationally advocate it for all five types of reason simultaneously. There has, however, been a general tendency for different advocates of energy efficiency to place the emphasis very differently.

The least radical reason for advocating energy efficiency – but the most widespread within governments – is as a means of *saving money*. Government expenditure has been put into policies to promote energy efficiency, and a return has resulted from this 'investment' in terms of money saved on energy. Private and corporate consumers have saved money, the public sector as a consumer of energy has saved money, and producers of electricity have been able to satisfy consumer demand without having to spend so much on building additional generating capacity. For the national economy as a whole, lower corporate expenditure on energy has reduced manufacturing costs and made exports less expensive to produce, whilst reduced expenditure on energy has been reflected in reduced expenditure on imports of energy, such as imported coal and oil. For both reasons, the balance of payments has tended to improve, and this has eased a constraint on macroeconomic policy, making it less dangerous to reflate the economy.

This is the conventional non-environmental rationale for energy efficiency policies, and it underlies many of the policies which governments have implemented in this area over the past twenty years. Such policies have generally been evaluated by comparing government expenditure on 'investment' in energy efficiency with the money saved as a result. This comparison gives a measurement of the 'cost-effectiveness' of different policies.

A second reason for advocating the promotion of energy efficiency is as a means of *reducing energy dependence*: the dependence of the economy on energy supplies. The efficient use of energy obviously tends to make energy consumption lower than it otherwise would be. There are at least three different versions of the view that this is a desirable outcome.

Energy supplies can be seen as running down, with disastrous implications for the world economy if this process continues unchecked. Energy efficiency cannot prevent supplies from being depleted, but it reduces the speed at which this happens. This argument is obviously more persuasive when applied to fossil fuels than to either nuclear or renewable sources of energy. There are difficulties about it, however, because scientific knowledge, the technology of mining and extraction, and increases in energy prices, can all create 'new resources', in the sense of resources that it becomes practically possible and economic to make use of. Energy consumption therefore has to be set against the 'new energy resources created' by scientific, technological, and economic change. Viewed in this light, fossil fuel supplies may not be running down at all, or else may be running down at a fairly slow pace, which can easily be compensated by the expansion of renewable and nuclear forms of energy.

Another version of the 'energy dependence' argument is that energy efficiency is a means of reducing the degree to which human beings become dependent on nuclear energy. For the reasons outlined in Chapter 1, the expansion of nuclear power is widely viewed as a dangerous process, and increased energy efficiency is one way to avoid it or slow it down.

Similarly, energy efficiency can also be viewed as a means of reducing dependence on imported oil. The world oil trade can be seen, because of its enormous scale and central importance for the world economy, as a destabilising factor in world politics and especially in the politics of the Middle East. The invasion of Kuwait and the war which followed is an example of the ways in which the economic importance of oil becomes combined with other causes of conflict, with large-scale military, human, and environmental implications. The world might be a safer place if the West depended less on the Middle East's oil. A long-term peacekeeping process might include not only the settlement of various ethnic and territorial conflicts, but also policies to reduce the West's energy dependence.

The third type of reason for advocating greater energy efficiency is the need to avoid a severe worsening of the greenhouse effect. The basic argument has already been outlined in the previous two chapters. Negotiations are currently (1992) taking place between governments with the aim of reaching an international agreement to restrain emissions of carbon dioxide and other greenhouse gases. If governments do reach such an agreement – or if they set their own unilateral targets for emissions reductions – they will need to have means of delivering on such commitments. Increased energy efficiency is one way in which they could achieve this.

Many of the policies which have been advocated as ways of combating the greenhouse effect – including Carbon Tax – would work partly by increasing energy efficiency. They have not been designed specifically to promote energy efficiency, however. That would simply be one of the ways in which these policies could be effective. Their primary goal is to curb carbon dioxide emissions, and this would be achieved through either increased energy efficiency *or* increased use of non-carbon-based energy (as a proportion of total energy consumed) *or* a reduction in the services derived from energy, or some combination of these.

A fourth way of seeing energy efficiency is as part of a general shift in the world economy towards *sustainability*. In this perspective, the carbon crisis is only one (though currently the most serious) of a set of existing and potential future crises affecting humanity's relationship with the various resources and cycles which underpin life on Earth. All resources, not only energy, need to be used efficiently, and all natural cycles, not only the carbon cycle, need to be maintained in balance. On this view, policies to promote energy efficiency are best seen as one part of a general overall process of 'greening' the world economy.

Energy efficiency would take its place in this process as simply one important example of a more general requirement for 'resource efficiency', i.e. the efficiency with which goods and services are produced from the various inputs used to produce them (labour productivity per hour is also an example of 'resource efficiency'). The analysis of 'subsidies in time and space' could be applied more widely than to energy alone, to consider in a much more general way the issues of intergenerational and international equity. Present efforts to reach international agreements about carbon dioxide emissions may prefigure a future general system in which a whole series of factors affecting the environment are kept within the limits of what the planet can sustain.[1] This might require a whole series of agreements between national governments, or perhaps some world-scale federal authority.

There has been a long debate over whether a world economy constrained in this way could continue with economic growth (which would have to be 'sustainable growth') – or whether it would have to halt the process of economic growth. Energy efficiency makes it possible to gain increased energy services (heat, refrigeration, the power to make cars move along, etc.) without an increase in the output of energy itself. It can therefore be seen as an example of 'squaring the circle', delivering growth in energy services whilst at the same time halting growth in the quantity of energy used.

It will, however, be difficult to achieve improvements in energy efficiency on the scale that would be required. Recent evidence is not encouraging. Total primary energy requirements in the 'West' – defined as the area of OECD countries – rose from 3,098 million tonnes of oil equivalent (MTOE) in 1970 to 3,887 MTOE in 1987, an increase of 25 per cent in 17 years.[2] This represents the resulting impact of factors tending to increase primary energy requirements – such as growth in manufacturing and transportation – together with factors tending to reduce requirements, including energy efficiency policies. Clearly the factors making for increased energy consumption have proved far stronger than those in the opposite direction.

The growth in primary energy requirements can be compared with other forms of growth during this period. The population of the OECD area grew from 714 million in 1970 to 819 million in 1987, a rise of 15 per cent.[3] Primary energy requirements per capita therefore rose. On an index with 1975 = 100, the OECD average in 1970 was 96 per head, and in 1987 the figure was 105.[4] Total Gross Domestic Product for OECD countries rose by 62.5 per cent between 1970 and 1987.[5] Therefore, whilst primary energy requirements as a whole rose, and requirements per person also rose, primary energy requirements per unit of GDP ('energy intensity') fell during this period. On an index with 1975 = 100, energy requirements per unit of GDP fell from 106 in 1970 to 82 in 1987.[6]

20

Although the environmental problems discussed earlier imply that this fall in energy intensity is good news, it is in fact much less significant than the overall rise in energy requirements. Whilst GDP growth over the period was 62.5 per cent, the fall in energy intensity was only 23 per cent. Only if the fall in energy intensity had matched the rise in GDP would energy requirements as a whole have stayed constant. The increase in energy requirements of 25 per cent was less than the increase in GDP but still a very large increase in the rate of energy consumption.

EVALUATING POLICIES

These four different rationales for increased energy efficiency – saving money, reducing energy dependence, combating the greenhouse effect, and moving towards a sustainable world economy – have different implications for efforts to evaluate policies to promote energy efficiency.

The 'saving money' rationale implies a fairly straightforward concept of 'cost-effectiveness': expenditure by government on policies to promote energy efficiency is compared with financial savings achieved from reductions in expenditure on energy.

The 'energy dependence' rationale implies that the effectiveness of energy efficiency policies should be judged by whether they do in fact achieve (or contribute to) a reduction in energy consumption (as a whole, or nuclear energy, or imported oil, depending on the particular version of the argument).

The 'greenhouse effect' and 'sustainable economy' rationales imply as a criterion the contribution made towards reducing carbon dioxide emissions. 'Cost-effectiveness' here would be measured in terms of tonnes of carbon emissions prevented per pound (or dollar etc.) spent on the policies. Problems involved in the attempt to measure environmental benefits in money terms by applying cost–benefit analysis to the greenhouse effect and global warming will be discussed in Appendix 1.

In general, environmental measurements of 'cost-effectiveness' (which are appropriate to the 'greenhouse effect' and 'sustainable economy' rationales) justify a wider range of policies, implemented on a larger and more costly scale, than are justified by the financial cost-effectiveness measurements which go along with the 'saving money' rationale.

EQUITY ARGUMENTS

Ultimately, however, the most important argument for promoting energy efficiency is that based on a fifth consideration, equity or fairness – both *intergenerational equity* (fairness between people in different generations) and *international equity* (fairness between people in different parts of the world).

Intergenerational equity is, in practice, effectively the same consideration as sustainability. Put at its simplest, if current generations destroy the global environment it won't be there for future generations to use. The more those of us alive today 'use up' the capacity of the Earth and its atmosphere to sustain life and economic activity, the less life and economic activity it will be possible to sustain in the future.

The exact implications of this principle for energy efficiency policy depend to a large extent on calculations of the degree to which the capacity of the atmosphere has in fact already been 'used up'. The Intergovernmental Panel on Climate Change (IPCC) Working Group 1, which investigated the rate and scale of climatic change, calculated that the concentration of carbon dioxide in the atmosphere in the future would only be held to the level it is at present if there are 'immediate reductions in emissions from human activities of *over 60 per cent*' of carbon dioxide and some other gases [my emphasis].[7]

> Atmospheric concentrations of the long-lived gases (carbon dioxide, nitrous oxide and the CFCs) adjust only slowly to changes in emissions. Continued emissions of these gases at present rates would commit us to increased concentrations for centuries ahead. The long-lived gases would require immediate reductions in emissions from human activities of over 60% to stabilise their concentrations at today's levels; methane would require a 15–20% reduction.[8]

International equity requires that those countries which have already consumed their fair share, or more than their fair share, of the Earth's capacity to sustain life and economic activity should make greater moves in the direction of energy conservation and efficiency than those countries which have up to now consumed far less than their fair share.[9]

This book is primarily concerned with energy efficiency policies in the member countries of the OECD, the Organisation for Economic Co-operation and Development. The OECD countries are: Canada, the United States of America, Japan, Australia, New Zealand, Austria, Belgium, Denmark, Finland, France, Germany, Greece, Iceland, Ireland, Italy, Luxembourg, The Netherlands, Norway, Portugal, Spain, Sweden, Switzerland, Turkey, The United Kingdom, and Yugoslavia. Most of these are countries which are consuming far more than their fair share of the atmosphere's capacity.

The OECD total population in 1986 was 813 million, out of a total world population of 4,917 million. The OECD therefore accounted for almost one-sixth of the world's people: 16.5 per cent.

In terms of energy consumption, the picture is a very different one. OECD total energy consumption was just over half of the world's total: 50.6 per cent.

It follows that five times as many people – those not in OECD countries – shared not quite as much energy as the OECD's inhabitants did. Energy consumption per head is therefore five times as high within the OECD as the average outside it.

Within the OECD part of the world, the USA accounted for almost half of the total, amounting to 24.4 per cent of total world energy consumption. The US population was 242 million, which is less than 5 per cent of the world total. US energy consumption in 1986 was more than nine times that of the whole of Africa, even though Africa's population was two and a half times that of the USA.[10] These differences in levels of energy consumption are reflected in similar types of differences in carbon emissions rates.

The high levels of energy consumption in OECD countries mean that improvements in energy efficiency here would have a major impact on energy consumption globally. Since OECD countries are generally in the lead technologically, with many of their innovations later being adopted elsewhere, technological improvements in energy efficiency in the OECD area may lead on to similar technological improvements elsewhere, therefore increasing the impact on global totals still further.

Starting from the IPCC minimum figure of a 60 per cent cut in world carbon emissions – which is the reduction necessary to stabilise concentrations in the atmosphere, and hence to stabilise the climate – it is possible to make some simple calculations about the implications for specific countries on the basis of international equity.

Michael Grubb quotes figures for the ratio of per capita emissions to the world average. These show that Japan and the European Community both had per capita emissions double the world average, USSR three times, and the USA five times the world average.[11] Since it is the world average which needs to be cut by 60 per cent, to 40 per cent of the current figure, the Japan/EC figure needs to be cut to 20 per cent of what it is currently (i.e. a cut of 80 per cent), the USSR/ CIS figure needs to be cut to 13 per cent of what it is currently (a cut of 87 per cent), and the US figure should be cut to 8 per cent of what it is now (a cut of 92 per cent).

Figures specifically for the UK can be calculated from a table for carbon emissions per capita for 1987, which appeared in *State of the World 1990*. This gives 1.08 tons as the world average, making a reduction to 0.43 tons the figure necessary for a stable climate. The UK figure is given as 2.73 tons per capita.[12] Since 0.43 is 16 per cent of 2.73, the reduction required for the UK on the basis of international equity is 84 per cent off current emission levels.

These figures make no allowance for the fact that the IPCC saw their 60 per cent figure as a minimum, with 80 per cent at the top of their range; they make no allowance for the fact that 'carbon sinks' are provided by forests, which if taken into account in producing a figure for 'net emissions' of carbon reduce the per capita contribution of tropical Third World countries to the greenhouse effect below what is indicated by looking at 'gross' carbon emissions; and no allowance for the fact that the more energy-intensive countries have a record of past emissions which dwarfs the past emissions of less energy-intensive countries by more than is indicated by the ratio of current emissions. Taking any of these factors into account implies the need for even more drastic cuts in the richer and more energy-intensive countries than the figures quoted in the previous two paragraphs.

All this should be compared with the current UK government position of 'stabilising' emissions at 1990 levels by the year 2000 – which is a cut in emissions of exactly 0 per cent.

THE TECHNOLOGICAL POTENTIAL

Scientific American magazine in September 1989 gave some figures indicating the potential for energy efficiency improvements.[13] For example, the 'model average' for US cars was 18 miles per gallon, the 'new model average' was 27 miles per gallon, the best model 50 miles per gallon, and the best prototype 77 miles per gallon. This implies that for a journey of a given distance, the use of the best model instead of the model average would cut the number of gallons required by 64 per cent.

Similarly, in heating a home to a satisfactory level, the 'model average' required 190 thousand joules per square metre, the 'new model average' 110, the best model 68, and the best prototype 11. This also translates into a cut in energy use – when the best model replaces the model average – of 64 per cent.

Against these figures must be set three factors, one of which is that 'energy services demanded' may increase. In the case of home heating this is unlikely, because even the richest person doesn't want to be boiling hot all the time. Since there is a limit, in terms of temperature, to what consumers want, any improvement in efficiency is likely to lead to an almost equivalent fall in energy consumed. In the case of the car, however, cheaper car travel may well stimulate an increased desire for long journeys, and so efficiency improvement in this case is unlikely to bring an equivalent fall in the number of gallons of petrol used.

The second factor to be considered is that it takes time for the stock of homes, cars, industrial machinery, or anything else, to be replaced. People and firms are not going to rush out and buy the new model, throwing away what they already have, just because the new model is more energy efficient. It is likely that they will wait until what they have wears out and they need to buy a replacement, and then they may take energy efficiency into account in choosing the replacement. This makes it possible to turn figures for overall efficiency improvements into rates of efficiency improvement per year. For example, if it takes 10 years on average for something to be replaced, then in one year only one-tenth of the stock will be replaced, and so an overall cut of 64 per cent in energy requirements becomes a cut of 6.4 per cent in one year.

The third factor which is important here is that there is no inevitability about energy efficiency improvements being put into practice. Technological advances don't lead to advances in what consumers actually buy unless the price is right. In particular, the key relationship here is between the prices of the new model and other available models, and the price of energy. At a time of cheap energy, consumers are unlikely to spend a lot of extra money buying the most technologically advanced energy-efficient products.

What is actually being referred to when phrases like 'more energy-efficient technologies' are used? A recent study by the OECD and the International Energy Agency[14] included the following as examples of 'promising areas for technical development':

- Advanced road vehicle design, including reduced size and weight, and advanced engines.
- Improvement in energy efficiency of air conditioning.
- Use of heat pumps in buildings.
- Improved heat efficiency through highly efficient insulating materials.
- Windows which adjust opacity to maximise solar gain.
- Improved electromechanical drives and motors to increase efficiency in manufacturing machinery.

Scientific American, September 1990, includes a diagram of an energy-efficient room with its own energy-efficient lamps, a light sensor to adjust the lighting in response to changing daylight conditions, and an occupancy sensor to turn off the lights when there's no-one in the room.[15]

There is no shortage of ideas such as these in the field of energy-efficient design. If these ideas are to be put into practice on a large scale by firms and consumers, however, the right sorts of policies need to be in place, and at the centre of these policies must be a recognition that the atmosphere is a finite resource.

ENERGY TRENDS

Another part of the relevant background when considering energy efficiency policies is obviously past and current trends in energy use, energy intensity, and carbon emissions. Some key statistics are:

World energy use, 1890–1990

	1890	1910	1930	1950	1970	1990
World population (billions)	1.49	1.70	2.02	2.51	3.62	5.32
Total world energy use (terawatts*)	1.00	1.60	2.28	3.26	8.36	13.73

Source: J.P. Holdren, 'Energy in transition', *Scientific American*, September 1990, p. 112.

Note: *A terawatt is equivalent to a billion tons of coal or five billion barrels of oil per year.

World carbon dioxide emissions from fossil fuel use (and cement production), 1950–87

	1950	1960	1970	1980	1987
Millions of tonnes of carbon	1638	2586	4090	5263	5650

Source: World Resources Institute, World Resources 1990-91, Oxford, Oxford University Press, 1990, p. 350.

Carbon emissions for selected countries, 1988

Carbon emissions from fossil fuel use, in millions of tonnes, and per capita emissions in tons, in one year

	Total	Per capita
US	1,435	5.85
USSR	1,015	3.58
UK	164	2.92
EC	744	2.31
China	713	0.65
Japan	289	2.35
India	189	0.23

Source: M. Grubb, Energy Policies and the Greenhouse Effect, vol. 1, Aldershot, Dartmouth, p. 48.

Fuel use in OECD countries, 1970–87

Totals, and percentage shares of different sources of energy

	Total*	Solid fuels (%)	Oil (%)	Nat. gas (%)	Hydro (%)	Nuclear (%)
USA						
1970	1,563	21	42	33	4	<1
1973	1,742	21	44	30	4	1
1979	1,916	25	45	25	3	3
1985	1,792	24	40	25	5	6
1987	1,840	24	43	23	4	6
Japan						
1970	282	23	69	1	7	<1
1973	340	17	75	1	5	<1
1979	377	15	70	5	6	5
1985	372	20	55	10	6	9
1986 (est.)	380	18	56	10	5	11

	Total*	Solid fuels (%)	Oil (%)	Nat. gas (%)	Hydro (%)	Nuclear (%)
OECD-Europe						
1970	1,044	30	57	6	7	1
1973	1,197	23	59	10	6	1
1979	1,286	22	54	14	7	3
1985	1,236	20	46	16	8	10
1986 (est.)	1,277	20	44	15	7	11

Source: J.G. Clark, *The Political Economy of World Energy*, Hemel Hempstead, Harvester/Wheatsheaf, 1990, p. 232.

Note: *'Total' = Total Primary Energy Requirements in millions of tonnes of oil equivalent.

Energy productivity

US dollars of GDP produced per millions of tonnes of oil equivalent of energy.

This is Gross Domestic Product divided by Total Primary Energy Requirements.

	1970	1973	1980	1984	1985	1986 (est.)
USA	1,227	1,266	1,418	1,602	1,693	1,747
Japan	2,386	2,391	2,902	3,272	3,440	3,455
Germany	2,618	2,610	2,980	3,196	3,243	3,285
UK	2,136	2,261	2,653	2,924	2,905	2,922
France	3,038	2,998	3,378	3,582	3,572	3,499
Italy	2,528	2,472	2,805	2,960	2,937	3,010
OECD-Europe	2,581	2,552	2,849	3,038	3,059	3,088

Source: J.G. Clark, *The Political Economy of World Energy*, Hemel Hempstead, Harvester/Wheatsheaf, 1990, p. 260.

Energy consumption

Total final energy consumption (i.e. Total Primary Energy Requirements minus net losses in production and use) in selected OECD countries, in millions of tonnes of oil equivalent.

	Industry	*Transport*	*Other*
UK			
1973	71	31	51
1979	61	34	58
1984	44	36	54
1985	45	37	58
Germany			
1973	85	34	79
1979	85	41	87
1984	73	43	77
1985	72	43	81
Japan			
1973	158	41	52
1979	146	54	61
1984	129	57	66
1985	128	58	65
USA			
1973	514	411	497
1979	523	447	418
1984	448	442	402
1985	436	445	400

Source: J.G. Clark, *The Political Economy of World Energy*, Hemel Hempstead, Harvester/Wheatsheaf, 1990, p. 337.

4

TWENTY REASONS FOR ENERGY INEFFICIENCY

In order to understand and evaluate different types of energy efficiency policies, it is necessary to examine the subject from the 'opposite end': the policies and other factors which make for inefficiency in energy use. This chapter outlines a series of ways in which the markets for energy operate to favour energy inefficiency rather than efficiency and conservation.

Many of these 'inefficiency dynamics' would be described by some economists as 'distortions' in the market, but rather than try to draw a distinction between 'distortions' and the free play of market forces themselves – a distinction which it is often very difficult to draw in practice – the distinction I am concerned with here is between economic dynamics which favour energy efficiency and those which do not.

The factors tending towards inefficiency in energy use are grouped here into four categories: information problems, organisational problems, financial problems, and environment and dependence problems. For each type of problem, it seems likely that a different type of policy will be appropriate. Types of policies will be discussed in Chapter 5.

INFORMATION PROBLEMS

1 *Consumers are far better informed about the prices of consumer durables than about their energy efficiency* and the costs of running them. In many cases consumers would be willing to behave 'rationally' and save money, as well as energy, by paying for more efficient consumer durables thereby saving money on running costs, *if* they had the information relevant to such a choice. Often they lack such information. This militates against the conservation/efficiency

option, with consumers making their choices on the basis of the information they do have, or can easily obtain: which means, primarily, simply the price of the appliance, machine, or building being bought.

2 This tendency is encouraged by the relative *invisibility of some costs* even after the product has been bought. In particular, the cost of electricity and gas is often difficult for consumers to discover. In some cases, metering may not even distinguish between separate flats in a block or large house, and certainly is unlikely to distinguish between energy use by different appliances (electricity bills in the UK, for example, do not itemise the charges so that consumers can see how much they are paying to run each appliance), tariffs are often complex and therefore difficult to bear in mind when deciding on energy use, and bills may be paid automatically through direct debit, perhaps only annually. Consumer durable prices are lump sums, with no calculation involved (unless they are bought through hire purchase or other forms of borrowing at interest), but taking into account energy costs involves complex calculations, even including prediction of future energy prices. Getting information and making calculations takes time, trouble, and sometimes money. Consumers normally prefer to make their choices simply on the basis of whatever information is readily available.

3 *Consumers often rely on the manufacturers and government* to deal on their behalf with difficult technical issues, such as energy efficiency. They do not always expect to have to deal with these issues themselves, and usually lack the necessary knowledge and technical skills.

ORGANISATIONAL PROBLEMS

4 Governments often intervene to regulate energy suppliers in ways which force them to *confine themselves to energy supply* and not diversify into conservation and efficiency. Although it may make economic sense to an energy utility to avoid the costs involved in building and operating additional capacity, and instead to invest money in helping consumers reduce their demand through greater efficiency, they may have a statutory obligation simply to provide the additional capacity and may be excluded from the business of energy efficiency.

5 Even without such regulations in force, energy suppliers may

limit their own activities in similar ways simply through a lack of imagination and a *fixed conception* of their objectives.

6 *Governments themselves often consume energy in an inefficient way*, for a variety of reasons. This is often the case with publicly-owned buildings (such as council housing in Britain), public transport, and government administration itself.

7 The *'energy efficiency industry' is often fragmented and badly organised* and generally unable to compete on equal terms with the energy supply industries, which are usually far larger, better-funded, and more influential politically.

8 Corporations in both private and public sectors often distinguish sharply between *current and capital spending*. For example, 'current' spending necessary to keep things going (e.g. energy running costs) may be seen as fairly unavoidable, but 'capital' spending (which can include investment in energy efficiency) may be seen as an optional extra to be afforded only when additional funds are available. Comparing money spent on energy efficiency with savings made in running costs crosses the current/capital boundary, where different forms of accounting and decision-making may apply. This is particularly the case where capital spending is financed by borrowing, and borrowing is limited, as in the case of UK nationalised industries.

9 *Rented accommodation* creates particular problems, because investment in energy efficiency is not paid for by the same person as the one reaping the benefits of lower running costs. For example, a landlord may pay to insulate a flat, but it is the tenant who saves money on heating bills. It will be difficult to prove to new tenants that it is worth paying a higher rent because of the higher level of energy efficiency. Similarly, if the tenant invests in energy efficiency features, he or she may have moved out before the returns from efficiency pay back the investment, and the next tenant and/or the landlord will benefit instead. The same principle applies to owner-occupiers intending to sell and move house in the near future.

FINANCIAL PROBLEMS

10 One force which acts against efficiency in choices between more and less energy efficient options is the fact that *poorer consumers lack savings and may be unable to borrow* to finance expenditure on energy efficiency. They may be forced into what is often in fact the more expensive option – the cheaper product with much higher

running costs – because of lack of access to money. Since 'poorer consumers' in this sense are a substantial proportion of all consumers, this is a significant factor acting against overall energy efficiency.

11 *Standing charges* tend to reduce the financial benefit to the consumer from using less energy units, because standing charges are at a constant level regardless of the amount of energy consumed, and so money cannot be saved on them by consumers through energy efficiency.

12 Firms, and especially small firms, often lack the financial resources which would enable them to carry out the *Research and Development* necessary to develop, as producers, increasingly energy-efficient technologies.

13 The efficiency option in a situation of choice is also hindered by *short payback periods*. In most cases, opting for greater efficiency in the use of energy can be seen as a form of investment. This is because energy-efficient appliances, machinery, and buildings are usually more expensive to buy than their energy inefficient rivals or substitutes, but also cheaper to run. The extra cost of choosing the energy-efficient option brings a return in the form of lower energy bills over the years. The extra initial cost can therefore be compared with the total saving from lower bills over different periods of time.

It might be thought reasonable to compare costs over the whole period for which the product being bought would be in use, remembering that the returns from this investment should be compared with the returns from other possible investments (including putting the money in a bank), something which can be discovered roughly from the current going rate of interest. In practice, however, neither domestic nor industrial consumers appear to consider the whole time period of the life of the product, even where they have all the relevant information, but often confine themselves to simply the next few years, rejecting the efficiency option if the 'investment' is not paid for through energy savings achieved within that short time. A study published by Shell found that 'in industry, the maximum payback time allowed for cost-saving measures seems currently to be about 2 years only'.[1]

Michael Grubb reports that a 'study of the choices made by well-informed consumers in buying refrigerators which differed only in cost and efficiency concluded that only 40% of them bought the more efficient variety if it took more than 3 years to pay back (35% discount rate). Another 40% seemed to apply a discount rate above 60% (i.e. requiring payback in well under 2 years).'[2]

If energy suppliers – investing in new capacity in order to earn a return from energy sold – were to calculate their own investments on such a time-scale they would rarely if ever invest in any new capacity at all because it would only very rarely even be built within such a time period. The longer the time period being considered, the more likely it is that the result will be favourable to investment in efficiency. Short payback times favour energy inefficiency choices.

14 Governments often provide *subsidies for some forms of energy supply*, as with current UK policies maintaining a levy to subsidise nuclear power, or past UK policies of subsidising coal production. Unless matched by equally significant subsidies for conservation and energy efficiency, this is another source of bias in favour of extra supply of energy rather than investment to reduce demand.

15 Energy costs are often perceived by domestic and industrial consumers to be only a *small proportion of their total expenditure*, and therefore are not seen as something important to deal with when available time is limited.

16 *Taxes often discriminate* against energy conservation. For example, in the UK Value Added Tax is charged on energy conservation equipment but not on domestic fuel.

ENVIRONMENT AND DEPENDENCE PROBLEMS

17 Options which tend to increase the amount of energy consumed have a number of *effects on the environment* which efficiency/ conservation options do not have. These can be seen as 'costs' not paid by the consumers of the extra energy but paid by the environment (and hence by everybody, including members of future generations). Since the consumers themselves do not pay these costs (except to the extent that they suffer from the same environmental costs as everyone else), this represents a form of 'subsidy' – a subsidy taken from the environment and going to energy consumers. As with other subsidies, the effect is to reduce the price of the product (energy) below what it otherwise would be, and to increase the amount of it which is consumed. These subsidies from the environment therefore act against economising on energy use.

The main environmental costs of energy – or 'subsidies' for energy supply – were outlined in Chapter 1: acid pollution, the greenhouse effect, nuclear power station accidents, and radioactive waste. Also in this category we can place the proliferation of nuclear weapons which is resulting largely from the spread of nuclear power.

18 Other subsidies result from the importance of energy supply for the economy and society, and the dependence which this creates. The most important example of this is that *dependence on energy imports may lead governments into war*, threats of war, and preparations for possible war, in order to maintain their supplies. Military expenditure, loss of life by both the military and civilians, and environmental destruction caused by warfare, represent forms of subsidy for the supply of energy. There is nothing like an equivalent subsidy for conservation/efficiency options.

19 Dependence on imports of petroleum and other forms of energy can create *balance of payments* difficulties. Government policies to deal with these difficulties may cause other economic problems as a result, such as increases in involuntary unemployment, which can therefore in practice be another subsidy for energy consumption.

20 Finally, it is important to mention a further external cost which represents a large subsidy for current energy use rather than efficiency or conservation. *Depletion of fossil fuels reduces the resources which will be available to future generations*. In that sense, future generations are subsidising current generations if we use more than 'our share' of fossil fuel reserves. What 'our share' is depends primarily on how many generations it is right for reserves to be shared amongst. In a market economy, the pattern of consumer demand is shaped only by current consumers, and since unborn future generations have no current purchasing power, they are therefore unable to win for themselves their fair share of fossil fuels. Greater energy efficiency – through slowing down depletion rates – would help them to do so.

This chapter has outlined a series of subsidies and market dynamics which act against the choice of energy efficiency options. Two conclusions stand out. Firstly, in general, these subsidies and dynamics operate on a far larger scale than do government policies to promote energy efficiency, and are far more significant in their impact. Secondly, the barriers to energy efficiency are by no means entirely financial ones, and so it is therefore unlikely that Carbon Tax by itself will be sufficient to deal with all the barriers. In particular, the information and organisational problems need to be dealt with directly.

5

POLICIES FOR ENERGY EFFICIENCY

The causes of energy inefficiency discussed in the previous chapter are playing a large part in leading humanity to environmental disaster. This is despite the fact that many of them on their own don't look particularly serious, and others look like mistakes which are easily made and not really anyone's fault. Nevertheless, their total impact is to make a central contribution towards global warming, with the disastrous consequences outlined in Chapter 1. What at first sight look like fairly harmless economic factors turn out to be potentially catastrophic.

This chapter presents an overview of the different types of energy efficiency policies which have been implemented by governments in the OECD area in response to the causes of energy inefficiency during the period 1973–91. Policies of all these types could be used alongside Carbon Tax in the future.

PUBLICITY AND INFORMATION

General publicity campaigns have been used by governments to draw energy conservation and efficiency to the attention of the public. The UK government declared 1986 Energy Efficiency Year, and this included a large television advertising campaign in the autumn of that year. Japan has an Energy Conservation Month, with large-scale publicity, every year.

Governments have also made available much more specific information about energy costs, technologies, standards, etc. Energy audits have been provided to give consumers a detailed analysis of their energy use, combined with advice about cutting their consumption and hence their costs. In some cases, governments have provided audits themselves (e.g. Japan), in others they have subsidised the use of energy consultants (e.g. UK), or required gas and electricity utilities to provide audit services (e.g. USA).

Information can also be provided about the energy efficiency of electrical appliances and cars through labelling, booklets, and data published in advertisements. Technical manuals and handbooks have also been provided in some cases, along with technical advisory services, and training programmes such as the energy managers' programme in Japan.

An evaluation of the effectiveness of publicity and information campaigns, carried out by the OECD, was generally favourable, stressing the advantages of tailoring the information provided to the requirements of particular industries and groups of consumers.[1] There have, however, been some failures, such as the UK 'Lift a Finger' campaign in 1984, which was abandoned because of its ineffectiveness.

A further way in which information can be provided to consumers is through metering, especially where this enables consumers to find out about the rate of energy consumption and consequent costs involved in the use of different appliances. Recent developments in electronics have made it possible to improve the effectiveness of metering and meter displays.[2]

REGULATIONS AND STANDARDS

Governments can impose regulations on industry, buildings, and transportation, setting compulsory minimum standards for energy efficiency. For example, the Japanese government includes a requirement for an energy conservation plan to be submitted as part of its planning permission procedures for large buildings. The US government sets minimum standards for the fuel efficiency of new cars.

Some governments have introduced or supported voluntary schemes which enable manufacturers to advertise the fact that they have achieved particular standards. A voluntary agreement between the West German government and appliance manufacturers as a whole resulted in a 20 per cent improvement in efficiency between 1980 and 1985.[3]

An OECD study found regulations and standards policies generally useful, particularly in the case of regulations for buildings.[4] Regulating technologies used by industry has proved difficult, however, because of the enormous variety of technologies to be considered. Regulating domestic appliances is likely to be more effective, but this has not yet been tried on a large scale. Mandatory minimum standards make it possible to get round the problems caused by lack of adequate basic knowledge and expertise on the part of consumers. In that sense, they can be seen as an alternative to providing information, although of course both types of policies could be combined. Standards also have the advantage that they place little financial burden on governments.

Minimum standards fail, however, to provide any incentive for improving on them, and are therefore liable to become in practice maximum standards unless there is a consistent policy of gradually raising the minimum standards set, particularly where technical advances are making possible steady improvements in efficiency.

RESEARCH, DEVELOPMENT, AND DEMONSTRATION

Governments have also provided support for scientific research, technological development, and the diffusion of 'best practice' technologies. Western governments differ greatly in their general approaches to 'science policy', and these general differences are reflected in the specific policies they apply in this area of energy policy. Some countries, such as the USA, see the role of government as being primarily at the 'pure science' end, with the private sector responsible for its application. Others, such as Japan, pursue a much more active role for government at the 'applied' end of the scale.

In addition to scientific and technological research on energy efficiency, social science research has been carried out on consumer behaviour and the factors affecting it, such as demographic change, changes in consumer durables, and changes in energy prices.

Evaluations carried out on particular research, development, and demonstration policies have generally proved favourable in terms of the cost-effectiveness of government spending in this area.[5] There has, however, been a tendency to concentrate research on energy efficiency in industry rather than also to look into improving energy efficiency in consumer goods.

GOVERNMENT AS AN ENERGY CONSUMER

Governments themselves use energy, and can therefore have a direct impact on energy efficiency as well as using their own practices to set an example to other energy consumers.

The Danish government, for example, enforces energy efficiency standards for all public buildings. Low-energy building design can be applied to schools, hospitals, and government office buildings. In West Germany, a drive for greater energy efficiency within federal ministries reduced their energy consumption by 25 per cent between 1979 and 1983.[6]

Such policies have, on the whole, proved effective, although there can be difficulties in maintaining the momentum for further improvements after an initial set of improvements has already been achieved. The effectiveness of example-setting is obviously likely to be improved if combined with publicity and information about what has been achieved.

THE ORGANISATION OF ENERGY EFFICIENCY

Governments influence the ways in which the promotion of energy efficiency is organised, both directly through their own structures and indirectly through encouraging developments in the private and voluntary sectors.

For example, governments can encourage the formation of companies which provide energy management as a service to other companies; they give grants and other forms of support to voluntary organisations such as the German Housewives' Association in Germany and Neighbourhood Energy Action in the UK; they have also set up a variety of structures within government to co-ordinate and promote energy efficiency policies.

This area is one where evaluation is particularly difficult, and where much depends on the specific traditions and political situations in particular countries, including whether they have federal systems and what the state of relations is between the federal and state/regional governments.

Energy supply industries can be part of the structure for implementing energy efficiency, rather than simply concentrating on supply and leaving efficiency and conservation to other organisations. For example, many US states have regulations which require utilities to treat conservation as a 'fuel' in the sense of including it in their investment plans, financial accounting, and in the services they provide to consumers. It is in any case very often in the interests of utilities to reduce their own generating costs through promoting energy efficiency. This approach will be discussed in Chapter 7.

PRICING AND TAXATION POLICIES

Governments have considerable influence on levels of energy efficiency through their ability to affect energy prices by means of taxation, ownership and/or regulation of corporations supplying energy, and also at times through anti-monopoly, anti-inflation, regional, and trade policies.

Petroleum is generally taxed more heavily than other forms of energy. The primary objective of this taxation is usually revenue-raising rather than energy efficiency, but taxes which have the effect of increasing the prices of petroleum products tend to encourage efficiency in their use, whatever their intended objective.

Countries where there have been increases in petroleum taxation during the period 1985-7 include: Sweden, Denmark, Portugal, Australia, Ireland, Italy, Switzerland, and the UK. This was a period during which world crude oil prices fell, and so the effect of increased taxes wasn't necessarily to raise petroleum prices but often to keep them constant. This prevented falls in world crude oil prices from having the effect of drastically reducing levels of energy efficiency, but did little to positively promote increases in energy efficiency.

In some cases governments have subsidised or otherwise held down petroleum product prices. Examples of this are in Greece, Italy, and Portugal. There has been a general tendency during the 1980s to reduce or abolish such subsidies and controls, and this has presumably made some contribution to energy efficiency.

Coal is usually treated more favourably for tax purposes than petroleum is, and is often favoured by subsidies, controls on imports, and by the purchasing policies of electricity utilities (which may buy coal at above world prices from coal producers within the same country). Coal has been particularly favoured in Germany and (until fairly recently) the UK. In Sweden, however, coal taxation has been deliberately increased for efficiency and environmental reasons.

Gas has also been treated favourably for tax purposes in many cases, often with the aim of encouraging switching from imported oil to home-produced gas (e.g. policies in Australia, Denmark, and New Zealand).

For both gas and electricity there are complex issues about the ways in which pricing reflects the fixed and the variable costs, required rates of return from investment, and provision for peak consumption loads, etc. Decisions about pricing appear only rarely to have been influenced by energy efficiency and environmental considerations, however, though this has recently begun to change in some countries.

One general issue which affects both gas and electricity is whether tariffs are 'progressive' in the sense that prices rise as units consumed rise, or 'regressive', in the sense that prices per unit fall as consumption rises. For energy efficiency purposes, progressive tariffs – as in Japan – are preferable.

GRANTS, TAX INCENTIVES, AND LOANS

The costs of energy consumption are influenced not only by the price of energy itself but also by the prices of insulating materials, energy-efficient heating systems, energy surveys and audits, etc. (together with interest payments if the money for such investment is borrowed). These prices can be influenced by government policies as a means of subsidising and encouraging energy efficiency.

The main types of incentives are: grants (to industry and to residential users of energy), tax incentives, and loans. These have often been combined with information and publicity campaigns designed to ensure that energy consumers know about the range of incentives available.

Industrial grant systems have varied enormously in their details. In some cases, such as the Canadian Atlantic Energy Conservation Investment Programme, projects with longer payback periods have attracted higher levels of grants. In other cases, such as in Denmark, the grants depend on the ratio of investment cost and energy savings.

Residential grants have usually been for insulation and weather-stripping. In some cases, grants have been given only to low-income groups (e.g. USA) or only for rented accommodation (Netherlands and Sweden).

Tax incentives have been used in similar ways to grants to promote energy efficiency by both industrial and residential users. For example, in Belgium up to 20 per cent of energy conservation investment by companies is tax-free.

Loans by government at below the market rate of interest ('soft loans') have also been used. For example, the Swedish government gives soft loans to promote the construction of energy-efficient buildings, and the Dutch government uses them to promote Combined Heat and Power (CHP) district heating schemes. Loans are less widespread than grants and tax incentives.

An OECD study found that grants were generally more cost-effective than tax incentives and loans, though they were often complex and expensive to administer. They have been particularly cost-effective where they have been particularly selective in their eligibility criteria (as in the Canadian and Danish industrial grant systems). Residential grants have usually not worked well for rented accommodation, where landlords usually pay the cost of investing in energy efficiency, but it is tenants who gain the financial benefits. Financial incentives have proved more effective when combined with information and publicity.[7]

WHICH POLICIES WORK BEST?

This chapter has outlined some ways of combating and reversing the causes of energy inefficiency identified in the previous chapter. Some policies – such as the provision of information – can work in the context of existing prices for energy and existing required payback periods. Other policies, such as shifting the cost of investment in energy efficiency from consumers to energy efficiency firms (who can also be the energy suppliers), are able to change the required payback periods but again can work in the context of existing energy prices. Policies to end or counteract subsidies obviously do not retain existing energy prices but are intended to change them.

How effective have these different types of policies been? The evaluation of the overall effectiveness of different specific types of energy efficiency policies is an extremely difficult task. Policies change and patterns of energy consumption change too, but in order to arrive at conclusions about effectiveness, it would be necessary to establish cause-and-effect connections. One way to do this is to calculate figures for what would have happened in the absence of the policies, compare them with what actually did happen, and attribute the difference to the effects of the policies. This assumes, of course, that the difference cannot be attributed to some other factor left out of the calculations. There are also problems deriving from the fact that all policies are implemented in particular contexts: it may not be clear whether some features of those contexts are essential for the policies to work, or whether they were irrelevant to the effectiveness of the policies.

It is also necessary to be careful when interpreting studies which focus on the issue of 'cost-effectiveness'. Where cost-effectiveness is in purely financial terms – concerned with the money saved by the consumer as a result of the more efficient use of energy – the non-financial environmental costs are excluded. Once environmental costs are included in some way, far more policies and projects are then likely to be counted as 'cost-effective'.

The OECD/IEA (International Energy Agency) report, *Energy Conservation in IEA Countries*, reviewed a number of studies of the effectiveness of energy efficiency policies. In general, the conclusion reached by the report was that energy efficiency policies have usually proved worth while, comparing the cost to government with the benefits in terms of energy costs saved. This conclusion would be very greatly reinforced if environmental impact were also to be taken into account.

When studies have compared different types of policies, the picture which emerges is much more complex than one which simply shows one type of policy to be more effective than another. There are many cases where the effectiveness of a policy depends on it being combined with another policy such as a publicity campaign to inform people of the existence of the scheme. Information and publicity campaigns themselves depend on prices being sufficiently high to enable governments to appeal successfully to people's self-interest when considering energy efficiency investments. Not all policies increase each other's effectiveness, however: for example, regulations setting minimum efficiency standards for electrical appliances are not likely to achieve so much if labelling and other forms of information for consumers are already in place as they would in the absence of such information already raising efficiency levels. A great deal obviously depends on the specific form the policy takes – e.g. if grants are provided, what the level of grant is, what the criteria applied are, how the grants are calculated, how they are administered, etc. The specific circumstances in which the policy is implemented (e.g. whether market prices for energy are rising or falling) are also important.

Despite these and other complexities, it is nevertheless possible to arrive at some general conclusions about the effectiveness of energy efficiency policies. The first conclusion is that a mixture of policies is best, rather than concentration on a single policy instrument. This is mainly because energy is consumed in so many different ways by so many different types of consumers that one type of policy by itself is unlikely to influence all of them effectively. In most cases, different types of policy appear to reinforce each other's effectiveness. For example, since consumers frequently lack sufficient information about energy pricing, technologies, and systems for managing energy use, information is a necessary back-up to virtually every other type of policy.

The second general conclusion is that the overall scale of the policies is more important than the issue of which specific policies are the most effective. Since most energy efficiency policies have worked to some extent, the top priority in policy formulation is not for a way of choosing between different types of policies but for an increase in the overall scale on which energy efficiency policies of practically all types are operated.

Improvements in energy efficiency have failed to keep pace with economic growth, which threatens to obliterate the benefits of efficiency policies. For example, increased fuel efficiency in cars is of little use if total car-miles travelled increase far faster. Here the issue is not growth in GDP as such, but growth in car use, in manufactured goods, in population, etc. These are the basic processes tending to increase energy consumption, and if they continue energy efficiency policies must be on a large enough scale to counteract them.

Although no precise figures are available for the total effect of energy efficiency policies in recent years, it is clear that their overall impact has been on a much smaller scale than that which is now required. Energy efficiency policies on the scale of recent years will not contribute enough to dealing with the problem of global warming.

In fairness to those who designed the energy efficiency policies of the 1970s and 1980s, however, it is important to emphasise that these policies were never intended to operate on the sort of scale implied by the greenhouse effect. They were intended to save money, reduce import bills, and reduce some of the need for new generating capacity: aims far more modest than protecting the planet from global warming. The greenhouse effect has introduced a new urgency into the issue of energy efficiency, taking its significance far beyond what it was thought to be in the 1970s and 1980s by those who designed the generally rather unambitious energy efficiency policies of that time.

6

UK POLICIES

Total energy consumption in the UK has varied comparatively little over the past 25 years. The significant changes in energy consumption which have occurred during that period have been in how the total has been made up. Energy consumed by industry has fallen, and energy consumed by transport has increased. North Sea oil has reduced the proportion of UK energy consumption met by imports. There has been a marked decline in consumption of energy from coal, and a rise in the consumption of energy from gas.[1] Carbon dioxide emissions have fallen slightly during this period.

This apparently relatively stable overall situation is, in its environmental impact, far from stable. A constant rate of carbon dioxide emissions per year produces – above a certain level of CO_2 which has already been exceeded – a rising quantity of total carbon dioxide in the atmosphere because that quantity reflects not just this year's emissions but also the emissions of previous years. 'No growth' – in this case, no growth in energy consumption and carbon emissions – will not deliver sustainability. Long-term environmental sustainability requires a drastic reduction in carbon emissions per year – estimated to be at least 60 per cent – and international equity combined with sustainability would require a still more drastic reduction for the UK. My calculation in Chapter 3 gave a figure of 84 per cent for the reduction required.

When judged on this scale, the policies intended by UK governments to promote energy efficiency have had only a marginal impact. This chapter outlines what these policies have been, and concludes by offering an explanation for their weakness. Chapter 8 will make recommendations for future UK policies.

There were really no UK energy efficiency policies until the oil price quadrupled in 1973. The UK then joined in the general trend in

OECD countries towards government promotion of conservation. The 1974 Building Regulations were the first in the UK to set significant thermal insulation requirements. Heating and lighting restrictions were introduced for non-domestic buildings, the motorway speed limit was reduced, the 'Save It' advertising campaign was launched, and a loan scheme for energy saving in industry was introduced.

The Labour government which took office in 1974, and in particular Tony Benn as Secretary of State for Energy (1975–9), took this policy a stage further with the announcement in 1977 – at a time of cuts in public expenditure plans in other areas – of a £450 million programme spread over four years, including a large-scale building insulation scheme, and a variety of small schemes, to provide advice, grants, tax allowances, demonstration projects for industry, and so on.

This interventionist policy did not survive for long following the election in 1979 of a Conservative government pledged to uphold free market principles. The implication of free market economics is that if investment in energy efficiency is cost-effective, firms and individuals will invest in it. At a time of rising energy prices, the operations of the market are likely to favour conservation, and this is in fact what happened following the rise in oil and other energy prices in 1973, and again in 1979. The 1979 price rise allowed the government to cut its expenditure on energy conservation and yet still see an increase in energy efficiency expenditure in the private sector. Free market policies and energy conservation were therefore able to go together in a way which would not have been possible had energy prices been falling.

The Department of Energy said in 1982: 'the explicit role of market prices in determining energy demand removes the need for a separate allowance for energy conservation'.[2] Not only did this policy save government money, but controls on the finance of nationalised industries brought in additional income for the public sector by forcing up gas and electricity prices – which further stimulated energy conservation efforts.

The two Conservative Energy ministers from 1979 to 1983 both supported the market approach: David Howell 1979–81 and Nigel Lawson 1981–3. In 1983, however, Nigel Lawson was replaced as Secretary of State by a far more interventionist minister, Peter Walker. The Energy Efficiency Office was set up, within the Department of Energy, before the end of that year. Peter Walker said that he believed the UK could go from the bottom to the top of the international energy efficiency league table within five years.

The main emphasis, however, was still on market forces.

> The Energy Efficiency Office considered that annual savings of at least 20 per cent might be achievable in each sector of the economy by 1995 . . . Of the total of £7,000 million a year, the Office calculated, on broad assumptions, that market forces might generate £5,040 million, leaving Government pro- grammes needing to stimulate £1,960 million.[3]

Walker launched a series of policies designed to achieve the £1,960 million a year target. Between 1983 and 1987 more than 20,000 senior business executives held meetings with ministers to discuss energy efficiency, and 1986 was declared Energy Efficiency Year, with a major publicity campaign.

> Schemes for industry and commerce provide assistance towards the cost of energy efficiency surveys, demonstration projects, monitoring, and research and development, including feasibility studies on combined heat and power or district heating. Regional energy efficiency officers provide help to companies and support for firms' energy managers, of whom there are some 10,000. An Energy Saver Show, aimed at domestic consumers, visited over 400 locations, including shopping cen- tres and home exhibitions throughout Britain, giving infor- mation and advice on energy efficiency in the home.
>
> Grants are available to householders for loft and water-tank insulation. The Energy Efficiency Office . . . gives grants tow- ards the establishment of community insulation projects and is helping to develop home energy audits – assessments of the degree of efficiency in a household's use of energy.[4]

A new shift in policy took place in 1987, with the replacement of Peter Walker as Secretary of State by Cecil Parkinson. This marked a return to the 'market forces' approach. Government expenditure on energy efficiency was cut. The Energy Efficiency Office (EEO) budget of £24.5 million in 1986–7 was reduced to £15 million in 1989–90. The Breakfast Special briefings of local business and public sector leaders, run by energy ministers between 1983 and 1987, were ended. The energy survey scheme for industry, in operation since 1976, was stopped. The government advertising campaign to promote energy saving ended in 1988. The Energy Efficiency Demonstration Scheme for industry, providing information about new techniques and technologies, begun in 1978, was closed in 1989. Home insulation grants were greatly reduced, as was the scale of community insulation projects.

PRIVATISATION

Cecil Parkinson's top priority was preparing the privatisation of the electricity industry. A commitment to privatise electricity was included in the Conservatives' 1987 manifesto, and following their victory at the general election, a Bill was introduced to give effect to this commitment. Energy efficiency and environmental consider-ations played very little part in the formulation of the government's plans or in the drafting of the Electricity Bill.

The Bill received its House of Commons second reading in December 1988. In May 1989, the government was defeated in the House of Lords on an amendment designed to encourage electricity suppliers to promote energy efficiency. Despite support for this principle from Conservative backbenchers, twenty-five of whom signed a Commons motion supporting it, the Lords' amendment was deleted when the Bill returned to the Commons, and the resulting Act of Parliament (July 1989) contained only an extremely weak pro-vision on energy efficiency. This gave the Director General of Electricity Supply power to promote energy efficiency solely through the provision of information and the setting of targets. The rules governing the Director General's regulatory powers do not take energy efficiency into account.

In fact, they do the opposite. Though promoting energy efficiency may still save electricity suppliers money on the expenditure side (through often being cheaper than investing in new generating capacity), on their income side, the Director General regulates the prices they charge in accordance with the formula 'RPI + $X - Y$': RPI is the Retail Price Index, the main measurement of inflation, Y takes into account differences between the overall inflation rate and changes in costs of electricity supply specifically, and X is a factor designed to encourage cost-cutting. The prices suppliers are allowed to charge therefore depend essentially on the costs of generating electricity, and so enable suppliers to recoup money spent on adding to energy supply, but not money spent on investment in energy efficiency. This introduces a clear anti-efficiency regulatory bias into a supposedly 'market' structure.[5]

Wholesale reorganisations of the electricity supply industry do not happen very often, and the timing of this particular reorganisation, coinciding with increased international concern about global warming, suggested that a major boost for energy efficiency was possible at the time. The Electricity Act proved instead to be a missed opportunity.

Since privatisation, the electricity supply companies have offered discounts of 10–25 per cent to large-scale users, and have as a result provided a strong incentive for many borderline consumers to consume additional electricity in order to qualify for a discount.

A GREENER AGENDA

Electricity privatisation represented part of the 'Thatcher agenda' begun in government in 1979. But at the same time as privatisation plans were being developed in detail in the late 1980s, a new 'green agenda' was starting to appear in mainstream politics (though too late to affect the privatisation plans). Mrs Thatcher again played a leading role, drawing particular attention to the greenhouse effect and global warming. In her speech to businessmen at the Royal Society in 1988, she said:

> We must heed the dangers posed by the Greenhouse Effect. We are still adding 3 billion tonnes of carbon dioxide to the atmosphere a year. To ignore this could expose us to climatic change whose dimensions and effects are unpredictable. So energy efficiency is crucial.[6]

Energy efficiency – seen from 1973 to 1988 primarily as a means of saving money – was back in favour, but this time as a means of saving the world, by combating the greenhouse effect. In July 1989, Parkinson was moved from the Department of Energy and at the same time Chris Patten became Secretary of State for the Environment, with a 'mandate' from Mrs Thatcher to pursue parts of the new green agenda, including energy efficiency. John Wakeham became the new Secretary of State for Energy, appearing not particularly committed to any specific policy approach but to pragmatic competence and juggling between carrying through electricity privatisation and supporting government policy on the greenhouse effect.

In April 1990, new Building Regulations were introduced to tighten up energy efficiency standards for new buildings in England and Wales.

As a result, a house built in 1990 will be 20 per cent more energy efficient than one constructed this year [1989] – which means that in its lifetime each average three-bedroom semi-detached will emit 100 tonnes of carbon dioxide less into the atmosphere.[7]

Nevertheless, these new regulations lagged a long way behind those in many other parts of Western Europe. Friends of the Earth described them as 'approximately at the standard Sweden was at in the 1930s'.[8]

In May 1990, the House of Commons Public Accounts Committee published a report on *National Energy Efficiency*. This was basically critical of the policies pursued by Cecil Parkinson. Reviewing plans to reduce the budget of the Energy Efficiency Office, the Committee commented:

> In view of the overall good record of the Energy Efficiency Office for value for money in this area, we asked the Department whether it would not be more sensible to increase its budget so as to increase the energy efficiency savings stimulated through its activities.[9]

The Committee criticised the lack of co-ordination between the EEO and areas of government outside the Department of Energy. In particular: 'We consider that the slow response of departments to the 1983 national energy efficiency campaign as regards their own use of energy was a poor example to the Nation.'[10]

September 1990 saw the publication of the government's Environment White Paper, *This Common Inheritance*. This set out the government's response to the green agenda, covering a wide range of issues, including global warming and energy policy. In a potentially important statement of principle, the White Paper said: 'Energy efficiency improvements are the cheapest and quickest way of combating the threat of global warming.'[11] The White Paper sets out some proposed

> measures to help to achieve the challenging target that the Government has announced that it is prepared to set for Britain, if other countries take similar action, of reversing the upward trend in emissions of carbon dioxide and stabilising them at 1990 levels by 2005.[12]

'The Government intends to develop further EEO services during

1991 to help energy users to get expert advice, specific to their circumstances, on the purchase, design, operation, and improvement of energy-using equipment and of buildings. This could include assistance with project management for smaller companies . . .'[13] Further changes in the Building Regulations are being considered, with the aim of including in them a requirement for buildings to be 'labelled' with information about their energy efficiency. 'The Energy Efficiency Office is introducing a new system of advice and grants for lower-income households in both public and private sector housing.' This is the Home Energy Efficiency Scheme.[14]

The UK government also announced their intention of arguing within the European Community for the EC to set up two voluntary systems (perhaps to be followed later by compulsory versions), one for a 'common scheme for energy efficiency labelling of electrical appliances', and the other for 'minimum standards for a wide range of appliances – for example central heating boilers, fridges, washing machines and industrial heating equipment'.[15]

Responding to criticisms of the Energy Efficiency Office from the Public Accounts Committee and others, the White Paper announced that a new ministerial committee would be set up to monitor and co-ordinate energy efficiency efforts across government departments and amongst energy users more generally. The committee will be holding public hearings on energy efficiency.

The White Paper also mentioned the key, and politically very difficult, issue of energy prices. Referring to the need for 'further measures' to be taken, it says:

> In the long term these will inevitably have to include increases in the relative prices of energy and fuel. This could be achieved by taxation or other means, such as tradeable permits . . . Long term measures affecting the relative price of energy can only sensibly be taken when competitor countries are prepared to take similar action . . . In the immediate future the reduction of inflation is of overriding importance. Given this, and our best assessment of how long it will take to achieve an international consensus, tax or other measures directly raising the relative price of energy outside the transport sector will not be introduced in the next few years.[16]

The White Paper was widely criticised for its timidity. The *Financial Times* commented: 'The British government's strategy for the environment, published yesterday, would have been an excellent example of forward thinking had it appeared five years ago over the signature of, say, Mr Nicholas Ridley [the previous Secretary of State for the Environment]. In today's context it amounts to the least that could be said during the run-up to a general election.' 'It dwells mainly on proposals previously enacted or announced; when it comes to plans for the future the best that can be said is that it is a compendium of muted declarations of hesitant intent.'[17]

An editorial in *The Daily Telegraph* said:

> A national energy efficiency programme would set in train measures to combat carbon dioxide emissions. But the Government has stopped short of last-minute changes to the electricity industry which, in privatised form, will depend on selling more energy . . . That position will have to change when an international convention on the climate becomes a reality. The target of stabilising carbon dioxide emissions by 2005, which is five years later than the European Commission seeks, seems almost designed to cause trouble; Mr Patten has failed to budge the Department of Energy from its generous energy-use forecasts.[18]

This target was later altered to 2000, bringing it into line with EC policy, but no policy changes have so far been announced to enable this new target to be met.

The private car turned out to be politically the most difficult of all the problems the government encountered in writing the White Paper. Although the government declared its hopes that the fuel efficiency of vehicles could be improved, the White Paper contains the statement of principle that 'the Government welcomes the continuing widening of car ownership as an important aspect of freedom and choice'.[19] The Department of Transport stood by its May 1989 projection of an increase in road traffic by 2025 of between 83 and 142 per cent.

CONCLUSIONS

The promotion of energy efficiency has never played a central role in UK energy policy. The most important reason for this is that the UK has large energy reserves of its own, including coal, oil, and natural gas. It therefore has less need than many other countries to import energy supplies, and so the argument that it is necessary to promote energy efficiency in order to reduce the dependence of the economy on imports of energy is weaker here than elsewhere. It also means that there are powerful vested interests within domestic politics favouring the expansion of the energy supply industries, whereas the power of the energy efficiency industry is extremely weak by comparison.

There are also two important additional political factors. One is the emphasis on 'free market' ideas in recent British politics, especially during Mrs Thatcher's governments (1979–90). This has militated against government intervention in the market to promote energy efficiency, with the exception of the provision of information which is seen as 'making the market work better.' The other influence is the relative weakness of green politics in the UK in comparison to many other Western European countries. Looking back, the timid 1990 Environment White Paper now appears to mark the highest point of green influence in UK politics, following little over a year after the 15 per cent vote for the Green Party in the UK elections for the European Parliament. Further advances for environmentalist policy ideas seem likely to depend in part on politicians' calculations of the electoral support which can be mobilised for such policies.

7

LEAST COST PLANNING

The problem of short required payback periods is one of the most significant barriers to investment in energy efficiency. Although this problem has in many cases been overcome through loans, grants, and other financial incentives, there is another approach which removes the problem completely. This chapter will consider how this approach has worked in recent years in the United States of America.

This chapter does not present a general survey of US energy efficiency policies but focuses simply on this one aspect. It would be misleading to imply that 'least cost planning' is the most important aspect of energy policy or energy use in the USA, because overall the US has a record of being profligate and inefficient in energy use, many US government policies act against energy efficiency, and the US position in recent negotiations on global warming has been obstructing those seeking effective action. The reason for highlighting least cost planning here, rather than these other aspects of US policy, is that it is an approach which has generated a whole series of constructive and useful policy ideas, most of which are applicable not only within the USA but in other countries too. It is important to examine these before reaching conclusions about how best to promote energy efficiency in Britain and elsewhere.

The 'Payback Problem' is that consumers are often discouraged from investing in improved energy efficiency by the length of time it takes for savings on energy bills to fully compensate for ('pay back') the sum invested. Both individual and corporate consumers are generally only willing to tolerate short payback times, of perhaps two years. Energy efficiency investment often takes much longer than that to produce financial gains for the consumer.

This problem can simply be abolished by switching the initiative from consumers to energy suppliers, so that it is the suppliers who invest in improved energy efficiency. It is conceivable, of course, that the suppliers too would also only be willing to tolerate fairly short payback periods, but in fact suppliers are already used to time-lags between deciding to invest in additional capacity and the point when additional capacity becomes operational, and then from that point to their investment being repaid through revenue from sales of the additional energy supplied. They are generally willing to tolerate similar time-lags for investment in energy efficiency because the two forms of investment are in fact close substitutes for each other. Energy suppliers have a choice in deciding where to invest, between investment in additional capacity, bringing a financial return later, and investment in energy efficiency, also bringing its financial return later. The more investment in energy efficiency is carried out, the lower the amount of investment in additional capacity that will be required. Investment in energy efficiency can therefore be seen as one form of investment alongside others, all having the same objective of delivering energy services (heating, lighting, refrigeration, etc.) to consumers, but achieving this by different methods.

For any profit-oriented energy supplier, this approach clearly makes financial sense, because profits will be lower than they could be if suppliers invest in expensive additional capacity (power stations, gas supply lines, etc.) when they could have produced the same energy services, and the same revenue from consumers, more cheaply by investing instead in energy efficiency improvements. Energy efficiency needs to be considered as one of the options for investment if profit is to be maximised.

The profit motive does not always operate fully, however. Energy suppliers may be public sector non profit-maximising organisations, aiming only to achieve a specified rate of return on investment, or to break even, or relying on government subsidies. Where energy suppliers are privately-owned, they may be regulated by government in ways which discourage investment in energy efficiency (as in the privatised UK electricity supply industry), or they may be geared to a simple routine of expanding capacity to match forecast expansion in demand, without fully considering improved energy efficiency as an option.

The electricity and gas supply industry of the USA is mainly privately owned, but also publicly regulated – often in ways which encourage full consideration of energy efficiency investment. US experience in this field provides a great deal of evidence about ways in which it is possible to avoid the Payback Problem and promote energy efficiency through combining the use of market mechanisms and the use of regulation.

Electricity in the USA is supplied by over 3,000 'utilities', regulated by 49 Public Utility Commissions, one for each state (except Nebraska, which has no privately owned utilities to regulate). There are three main types of electric utilities: 245 privately owned companies known as 'investor owned', accounting for about four-fifths of generating capacity; publicly owned utilities, including six owned by the federal government and 1,900 municipally owned; and 1,100 small co-operatively owned utilities.

The Public Utility Commissions (PUCs) are state bodies which regulate all utilities, including those supplying gas, electricity, telephones, water, and in some states also railways and road haulage. Each utility is granted a franchise giving it a monopoly in the supply of a particular service in a particular area, but with this monopoly position comes a series of legal obligations, according to which the utility must provide a reliable and non-discriminatory service at reasonable prices. The PUC's role is to ensure compliance with these obligations. This involves it in deciding what levels of prices, and what tariff structures, are reasonable in each particular case. Although most regulation is carried out at state level, there is also a Federal Energy Regulatory Commission (FERC), which regulates wholesale sales of electricity across state boundaries, and also has overall responsibility for the six federally owned utilities.

In many cases, PUCs use their regulatory powers to require electricity utilities to give full consideration to possible investments in energy efficiency. The details vary between different states as regards the specific requirements laid down by the PUCs, the methods by which these are enforced, and the ways in which they are reflected in the operations of the utilities themselves. Three specific examples will be outlined here: Texas, Wisconsin, and the Northwest Regional Power Planning Council.

Texas has had a history of weak regulation of utilities. This became a major issue in the 1982 election for the governorship of the state. The winning candidate, who became Governor White, introduced a new regulatory system, strengthening the Public Utility Commission of Texas. In 1983, the PUC introduced a new Energy Efficiency Rule, making it compulsory for electricity utilities to examine possibilities for investing in energy efficiency. Every two years, each utility with more than 20,000 residential consumers has to send the PUC a plan to improve energy efficiency. The PUC then uses its regulatory powers, including its controls over pricing, to reward good plans and to penalise utilities whose energy efficiency plans are judged to be unsatisfactory.

Utilities intending to invest in new electrical generating capacity are required to apply to the PUC for a Certificate of Convenience and Necessity. The Texas Public Utility Regulatory Act states that such certificates may only be granted if the PUC finds that a need for the new capacity is implied by its forecasts of future energy demand, if it 'is the best and most economical choice of technology, and that conservation and alternative energy sources cannot meet the need'.[1]

The Public Service Commission of Wisconsin (the Wisconsin PUC) also requires electricity utilities to submit plans every two years, but these cover the whole range of investment plans and demand forecasts. The Commission has the power to accept, reject, or require modifications to be made to these plans. Its objectives in doing so include avoidance of wasteful duplication of capacity by different utilities in the state, and ensuring that investment in energy efficiency is considered on the same basis as investment in new capacity, with preference given to whichever are the most cost-effective options.

This approach developed out of public debate about plans in 1976 to build seven new nuclear power stations in Wisconsin. Anti-nuclear organisations put forward investment in energy efficiency as an alternative. This option is now systematically included in the planning process as a matter of course.

The Northwest Regional Power Planning Council was set up by Act of Congress in 1980. The Council considers energy requirements and possible means of meeting them in the Pacific Northwest region. The Act specifies that utilities will only be allowed to construct new generating capacity if consumer demand can be met neither through conservation measures nor by renewable sources of energy. The Council's 1983 plan says:

> Conservation is treated as a resource. This means that the Council has taken great care to analyse conservation as a substitute for additional electric generation. Conservation is included as an additional supply of electricity rather than as a reduction to the demand growth forecast.[2]

Demand is forecast on the basis of predicted future levels of energy efficiency, with investment to produce additional improvements in energy efficiency being analysed as a method of satisfying that demand, comparable with other forms of investment designed to achieve that same objective.

Many of the regulatory bodies hold semi-judicial public hearings to enable open debate to take place on the merits of different ways of supplying energy services. Some PUCs, such as the California PUC, are divided into two parts: one to act as advocates for the public interest, and one to reach impartial decisions on the basis of the arguments presented by all sides. In some cases, PUC Commissioners are elected, but in most cases they are appointed by the state governor (subject to approval by the state legislature).

The overall effect of PUC activities is to introduce pressures which in some respects act as a substitute for competition, and also to produce an element of competition within utilities between the options of expanding capacity and increasing efficiency. This system of public regulation creates a framework within which advocates of a variety of energy efficiency measures can put forward their arguments. In eight states, there are open auctions between organisations willing to sign contracts to supply or save electricity, with the states choosing the cheapest bid. This is known as 'all-source bidding'.

The types of measures put into operation by utilities include: home energy audits, free insulation for low income consumers, rebates for consumers who buy new and more energy efficient products, and (as in California) the supply of free hot water cylinder jackets and energy-efficient shower heads.

For example, the Pacific Gas and Electric Company, the largest investor-owned utility in the USA, under pressure from the California PUC, offers all residential consumers a free energy survey of their home, with zero-interest loans for the installation of measures recommended by the survey and free basic conservation measures, such as minor roof and window repairs, for low income consumers. The Company also provides rebates to people who replace their existing appliances by more energy-efficient ones.

New England Electric compensates developers by paying them the extra cost of installing energy-efficient equipment in their buildings, and offers to install efficient lighting and heating in existing commercial and industrial buildings. The regulators allow New England Electric to keep 20 per cent of the savings achieved, which gives them a higher rate of return than they could achieve from investing in extra generating plant. Seven states operate a 'feebate' system, whereby developers of new buildings either pay a fee or receive a rebate when they connect to the grid, depending on how energy-efficient the building is. The fees pay for the rebates, so there is no net cost to taxpayers.

The Payback Problem is automatically overcome to the degree that responsibility for expenditure on energy efficiency is shifted away from consumers and over to the utilities. Where efficiency measures are provided free by the utilities, there is obviously no problem at all for consumers about payback periods. Where efficiency measures do require some expenditure from consumers, the Payback Problem can still exist, though it is in a much less serious form if audits, financial subsidies, and other forms of assistance, are provided.

THIRD PARTY FINANCE

Another way of overcoming the Payback Problem is to shift the responsibility for expenditure on energy efficiency from the consumer to a 'third party' (i.e. neither the consumer nor the utility). The USA provides many examples of this approach in operation. In fact, many of these 'third parties' are subsidiaries owned by gas and electricity utilities.

Consumers can enter into an agreement with a third party for an energy audit to be carried out, and then for various energy efficiency improvements to be introduced. The third party can then charge consumers for these improvements over a period of time, whilst consumers are simultaneously gaining the benefit of a reduction in gas and electricity bills rather than having to pay for energy efficiency in a lump sum at the time an improvement is first made and before any benefits are gained.

In some cases, the third party guarantees a particular level of savings for consumers and itself takes the risk that it may not be able to achieve these through the efficiency improvements it introduces. There can also be agreements whereby any savings made are shared between the consumer and the third party. One such agreement was reached between New York City and Benec Industries, whereby Benec improved the energy efficiency of 27 blocks of municipally-owned flats by installing insulation, boiler modifications, computer monitoring equipment, etc. The heating bills, which are paid by the City, were reduced as a result, with savings being shared between New York City and Benec.

Agreements can also be reached between utilities and third parties. For example, the Bonneville Power Administration (which is regulated by the Northwest Regional Power Planning Council) buys in energy savings from energy service companies, which install and finance efficiency improvements. The company is paid for the savings achieved, and the savings enable the utility to reduce the costs of generating electricity below what it otherwise would be.

EFFECTIVENESS

How effective are these approaches? A study by the State Government of Michigan, completed in September 1987, 'concluded that "aggressive" implementation of demand-side programmes, independent of any efficiency improvements induced by changes in electricity prices or other energy market conditions, could reduce electricity demand in the year 2005 by about 8% with peak load reductions of 8.5–8.7%.'[3] Other recent US studies 'suggest that the rate of electricity demand growth could be slowed by 0.6–1.8 % per year over a period of roughly ten to twenty years with the intervention of utilities and governments to further the adoption of cost-effective measures to improve efficiency (or manage load)'.[4]

The types of policies described in this chapter do appear to make a significant difference to levels of energy demand. It is necessary, however, to qualify this statement in a number of different respects.

Firstly, not all Public Utility Commissions operate these policies (in 1988, 29 out of 49 did)[5], and where they do they differ in the degree of enthusiasm and funding with which they are carried through. A survey by the Investor Responsibility Research Center in Washington, DC, covering 88 private utilities and 35 publicly-owned utilities found that 'only seven utilities accounted for 70% of the total funds spent' on energy efficiency and renewable energy programmes.[6] The implication of this is that far greater savings than those which are currently made could be achieved if well-funded energy efficiency programmes were in operation throughout the whole of the USA.

Secondly, the majority of examples of successful policies are in the electricity industry, not in gas. The structure of the US gas industry separates original gas supply, pipelines, and distribution to consumers, each of which are in the hands of different companies. This makes energy efficiency measures much more difficult to organise than is the case where there is vertical integration right through from original supply to the consumer, as in the electricity industry in the USA and gas in Britain. Again, the implication is that there is potential for further savings to be made if ways can be found to apply these policies to the US gas industry.

Thirdly, there is evidence of an economic bias in consumers' responses to energy efficiency policies. Better-off consumers are naturally in a better position to follow up home energy audits with expenditure on efficiency improvements. For free audits to be effective with all consumers they need to be combined with zero-interest loans or other financial incentives for expenditure on energy efficiency. Free home energy audits on their own don't make a large impact.[7]

Perhaps the most important issue for the purposes of this study, however, is whether the USA is in some way a special case, so that its policies could not be successfully transferred to the UK and other countries. Obviously the structure of the gas and electricity industries and their regulation are different in the US and the UK, but any problems from this source could be remedied by policy changes, such as changes in the UK guidelines for regulation.

More significantly, the US does have particularly high costs of new capacity.[8] This means that where new capacity and energy efficiency measures are treated as comparable forms of investment, energy efficiency very often turns out to be more cost-effective. Outside the US, however, where the costs of new capacity are generally lower, a system which selects the cheapest option would more often produce investment in new capacity than is the case in the US. The 'least cost' solution is not necessarily always going to be energy efficiency, and is in fact less likely to be energy efficiency in the UK than it is in the USA.

Nevertheless, if the concept of 'least cost' is expanded to include not only financial costs but also environmental costs – such as the contribution which fossil fuel use makes to the greenhouse effect – then energy efficiency options become attractive in practically all countries. It is also clear that energy efficiency has a much better chance of being the selected option where it is considered systematically alongside other investment plans than it does where it is regarded as a marginal extra. And since the utilities deal with all consumers directly, they are in the best position to introduce energy efficiency measures on a comprehensive basis. Overall, US 'least cost' policies have a great deal to contribute in the area of overcoming the Payback Problem and improving the efficiency of energy use.

8

POLICY CONCLUSIONS

In formulating a set of policy recommendations, there are six issues in particular which have been highlighted and require some sort of response. The first two of these were discussed in Chapter 1, the others in Chapter 2.

1 Sharing many of the same causes as the greenhouse effect, there is the related problem of acid rain and other forms of acid pollution. Policies designed to deal with the greenhouse effect may not adequately deal with acid pollution.

2 Carbon Tax proposals carry with them the danger that a major consequence will be a shift away from carbon-based fuels to nuclear energy. Despite the urgency of the greenhouse effect, it is important not to forget the problems of nuclear power, and so ways should be found to compensate for the impact that Carbon Tax will have in strengthening the economics of the nuclear industry.

3 Carbon Tax cannot possibly deal with all the 'non-price problems' which stand in the way of the more efficient use of energy. The record of energy efficiency policies in OECD countries over the past twenty years has a lot to tell us about ways in which these non-price influences can be responded to.

4 A flat-rate Carbon Tax would hit the poor more than the rich, because poorer people generally spend a much higher proportion of their incomes on domestic fuel than richer people do.

5 The price elasticity of demand for carbon-based fossil fuels is not straightforward, and so it is difficult to predict the impact of different rates of Carbon Tax on consumer demand for different forms of energy.

6 Some versions of Carbon Tax would have an adverse macroeconomic impact on the countries introducing them, tending to

worsen their balance of payments, unemployment, and inflation rates.

This chapter attempts to respond to these six problems by formulating a set of recommended policies (numbered 1–15) to be introduced alongside Carbon Tax, and a particular version of Carbon Tax itself. I shall consider each of the six problems in turn, and then discuss some of the wider issues involved.

ACID POLLUTION AND NUCLEAR POWER

The same argument which implies that there is a need for a Carbon Tax also holds good for the problems of acid pollution and nuclear power, implying the need for taxes against these too. There could therefore be: *(1) an Acid Pollution Tax* and, more importantly, also *(2) a Radioactivity Tax*, to ensure that Carbon Tax does not produce a switch over to nuclear power.

An alternative to introducing a Radioactivity Tax at the same time as a Carbon Tax would be a general Energy Tax, or hybrid Carbon/ Energy Tax, applying to nuclear power along with the fossil fuels, and combined with subsidies for renewable sources of energy. Depending on the details of these taxes, this could have the same effects, making nuclear-generated electricity and fossil fuels more expensive, and favouring both renewable energy and conservation.

A full set of policies in response to the issues raised by nuclear power is outside the scope of this book, but in addition to tax policies it is also particularly important to introduce much stricter international controls on the production and use of nuclear materials in order to combat the danger of nuclear proliferation which threatens to make the post-Cold War era even more dangerous than the Cold War era was.

Carbon Tax could become part of a general shift towards encouraging greater resource efficiency through taxes on the use of resources. Some people have proposed that resource taxes should replace income tax, but this would remove an important progressive element in the tax system and hence be regressive in its impact. It would be better to adopt the principle of 'tax inputs, not outputs', so that taxes on energy and other resources would replace sales taxes such as Value Added Tax, rather than replacing income tax.

NON-PRICE PROBLEMS

Amongst the energy efficiency policies of OECD countries over the past twenty years are policies to deal with practically all of the non-price barriers to energy efficiency. Here I will just briefly mention the types of policies involved (see Chapter 5 for more details).

(3) Publicity and information campaigns to inform energy users about the energy efficiency and running costs of particular products and buildings, about methods of managing energy use, and about the general importance of energy efficiency. The provision of fuller information should include energy audits, improved metering, and requirements for manufacturers (as well as government) to provide information – for instance, by labelling of domestic appliances and cars.

(4) Minimum standards of efficiency in energy use should be laid down by legislation and raised from current levels, especially for cars and buildings. These standards should be raised further in future years.

(5) Public sector energy efficiency should be improved, especially in public buildings, council housing, and public transport.

(6) The organisation of energy efficiency provision should be improved, including the incorporation of energy efficiency consider-ations into planning by organisations primarily concerned with energy supply – adopting the principles of 'least cost planning' and 'Third Party Finance' (see Chapter 7).

(7) Grants, tax incentives, and loans should be used to promote energy efficiency. In many cases, however, they will be less appropri-ate than Carbon Tax and so should be used when there is particular difficulty about the availability of finance for investing in energy efficiency. This applies especially to poorer domestic consumers. There is also a specific need for government subsidy to encourage research and development in the energy efficiency field, because this produces benefits much more widely than simply to the firm or institution carrying out the research and development. Government should provide increased support for the diffusion of 'best practice' technologies. Specific schemes should be introduced to subsidise energy efficiency expenditure in rented accommodation.

THE DISTRIBUTIONAL PROBLEM

The impact of Carbon Tax on poorer people implies the need for two different types of policies: compensation to go alongside Carbon Tax, and a particular version of Carbon Tax.

(8) Energy efficiency help for poorer consumers. Government should ensure that the tendency which Carbon Tax has to increase the energy costs of poorer domestic consumers should be compensated by help to those consumers to improve the efficiency of their energy use, thus achieving the twin objectives of bringing about an improvement in the energy efficiency of millions of consumers and at the same time ensuring that poorer people don't lose out in the process. Government help could be financed by revenue from Carbon Tax, and this would be a way of preventing Carbon Tax from having a deflationary impact. Help for poorer consumers could take a variety of forms, including free advice and energy auditing, the provision of free house insulation, access to grants, and assistance with making applications for grants.[1] Standing charges in fuel bills should be abolished.

(9) Progressive Carbon Tax. The rate of Carbon Tax should vary, not only according to the carbon content of a fuel but also according to the quantity used, so that it is charged at a higher rate as the quantity used increases. This would apply to domestic electricity and gas, with Carbon Tax on petrol, paraffin, and for the corporate and public sectors being charged at a flat rate.

The Progressive Carbon Tax (PCT) would make Carbon Tax operate on the same basis as income tax, where it is not simply the tax paid which increases as income increases, but also the tax rate per pound which increases. In the case of Carbon Tax, it would be administratively very difficult to make tax rates payable dependent on income, but they could easily be made dependent on quantity of energy used. It would be a simple matter for bills for electricity and gas to charge domestic consumers at different rates according to the quantity of fuel used during the quarterly period.

A problem with this policy is that it could encourage consumers to switch to a diversity of fuel supplies, so that consumers of large quantities of fuel would seek to cut down their fuel bills by installing gas, electricity, paraffin, etc., rather than just relying on a single fuel source. The effectiveness of this method of avoiding the progressive principle of the tax would be limited by the limited range of possible fuel sources which could be used (except for renewable sources, which the Carbon Tax policy is designed to encourage anyway). It could also be limited by linking together electricity and gas billing, so that the tax rate charged depends on the combined quantity used of the two fuels.

THE ELASTICITY PROBLEM

There are really two different problems about setting the appropriate particular level of Carbon Tax. One is not knowing what the price elasticity of demand will turn out to be. The other is having to charge a very high rate of tax because the elasticity of demand turns out to be very low, i.e. consumers have a very low degree of responsiveness to the price increase produced by the tax. Policies are needed to deal with both these aspects of 'the elasticity problem'.

The only appropriate responses to uncertainty about the elasticity of demand must surely be more thorough research into elasticity of demand and, more importantly, a willingness on the part of government to *(10) adjust tax levels* as information becomes available through the actual experience of Carbon Tax and consumer responses to it. The tax needs to be set initially at the level implied by the best estimates available and varied thereafter in accordance with new information, changes in consumer response, and new technological developments.

At the same time, efforts should be made to increase the elasticity so that lower rates of Carbon Tax are required than would otherwise be necessary, or so that existing rates can have more impact on carbon emissions. The types of policies outlined under the headings 'non-price problems' and 'energy efficiency help for poorer consumers' should all have the effect of increasing consumer elasticity. Other types of policies which would be likely to achieve that include *(11) greater government promotion of renewable sources of energy,* including research and development in this field. This would make it easier for consumers to switch out of carbon-based fuels. There should also be *(12) greater government investment in public transport,* to make it easier for consumers to switch away from the use of private cars.

MACROECONOMIC IMPACT

The uncertain macroeconomic impact of Carbon Tax similarly implies the need both for thorough research and a willingness to adjust tax rates. In addition, three other types of policies should be introduced to moderate the macroeconomic impact of the tax, limiting any tendency for unemployment, inflation, and imports to rise.

(13) Revenues from Carbon Tax should be 'recycled' through government expenditure. Expenditure would in any case be required for many of the policies already outlined, such as greater investment in public transport and help for poorer consumers.

(14) Carbon Tax should be charged on imports, so that imported goods and services from countries without Carbon Tax do not have an unfair advantage when competing against home-produced goods and services which have been made more expensive by Carbon Tax. No discrimination against imports would be required here, simply taxation on an equal basis. There might similarly be rebates on Carbon Tax charged on exported goods going to countries without their own Carbon Tax.

(15) Carbon Tax should be spread through international agreement. Carbon Tax is designed to deal with a global problem, and it will obviously be more effective the more global it is in its scope. Countries, particularly small countries, which introduce their own Carbon Tax have to cope with the problems of Carbon Tax whilst having only a relatively small return from it in the form of a slight tendency for the greenhouse effect to worsen at a slower rate. There will be a much more tangible return from Carbon Tax when it is implemented on a large scale, perhaps through agreement within the European Community, and then agreement between the EC and the USA. The main barrier at the moment to the spread of Carbon Tax internationally is the policy of the US government, though there is political pressure within the USA for this to change.

TOWARDS AN ENERGY-EFFICIENT SOCIETY

Policies to promote energy efficiency should be combined with other types of policies which can also contribute towards a reduction in greenhouse gas emissions.

For example, in addition to greater energy efficiency in car design there should also be policies to encourage reduced car use, including improvements in public transport and reforms in land-use planning. Land-use planning should take full account of energy considerations in decisions about where to site housing, workplaces, shopping, and other facilities. The aim should be to reduce the overall need for transport, especially private car use.

The '4Rs' should be encouraged: recycling, re-use, repair, and reconditioning. These would all help to reduce energy use and carbon emissions. Energy that is consumed should increasingly be from renewable sources such as solar power and wind power. It is also important to maintain 'sinks' for carbon, such as tropical rainforests.

As these examples suggest, a much wider set of policies can contribute to the reduction of greenhouse gas emissions than simply energy efficiency policies of the sorts discussed in this book. Energy efficiency does, however, have a major contribution to make.

POLITICAL WILL AND POLITICAL CULTURE

The carbon crisis is serious. It is part of the general evolutionary crisis of the relationship between our own species and the rest of the planet. As with many other aspects of this general crisis, there are clear and specific policies which could be implemented to deal with the problem. They would be straightforward to finance and to administer.

There is, however, one aspect which is far from straightforward, and because of this there would be something very unsatisfactory about ending this book simply with a series of policy conclusions. Important though it is to be careful about the choice of specific policies, just to leave it at that and hand the task of implementation over to politicians is to miss some of the more fundamental issues at stake.

However persuasive research about policy recommendations may be, and however heroically political leaders may summon up the much-sought-after quality of 'political will', they will not survive in office for long unless there is either a dictatorship or a widespread desire to support the types of policies they are seeking to implement. In a society which is to some degree a democracy, the key factor is the general political culture – the basic mix of attitudes which determines which sorts of policies are acceptable to people and which are not.

In many cases, energy efficiency policies have clear practical and financial advantages for individuals calculating their own self-interest. But other policies, such as high rates of Carbon Tax, go beyond that because they depend essentially on a wider sense of responsibility than merely individual self-interest. An important part of politics is the evoking, articulation, and mobilisation of wider senses of responsibility. Perhaps the clearest example of this in recent times has been nationalism. Millions of people have risked their lives, not out of a sense of their own self-interest but out of their sense of identification with the nation as a whole and their sense of sharing responsibility for its future. In the case of energy efficiency, there is no requirement for people to risk their lives, merely to be prepared to vote for politicians who say they will put up the prices of petrol and electricity. But nationalism may offer some clue as to how people might be persuaded to act against what looks like their own short-term self-interest.

Nationalism is about a sense of identification with something larger than the individual. What is needed now is a widening of that sense of identification to encompass the even larger unit of the planet as a whole. Whereas the nation-state is to a great extent an artificial construction which has had to be deliberately created, in many countries only very recently, the planet is a real physical and biological entity which has existed for billions of years. If it is possible for so many people to make so many sacrifices for an artificial construction, it should be possible for much smaller sacrifices to be accepted for something which has a real existence and on which so much else depends.

The current combination of resurgent ethnic rivalries and potential ecological disasters implies that much of the politics of the end of this century and the beginning of the next will be about the ways in which nationalism and a new developing 'patriotism of the planet' might work together, and about the tensions between them.

In Chapter 2, I referred to the 'triple subsidy' which present-day inhabitants of OECD countries receive from the people of the world's South, from future generations of all countries, and from the past. Coping with an end to that triple subsidy depends on a widening of the sense of political identification – a widening in terms of space, from nation to planet, and a widening in terms of time as well.

Current Western societies appear to be exceptional in the weakness of our sense of continuity through time. Much of politics is taken up by a frenetic series of responses to what is in the daily newspapers and hourly news bulletins. The working lives of politicians are not organised in ways which encourage them to take a long-term view of things (though this may happen when they retire). In contrast, however, there is a desperate need for political representatives who both think long-term and encourage society as a whole to think long-term. Much more is required than simply the very easy-sounding 'implementation of policies'.

Appendix 1

GLOBAL WARMING AND COST–BENEFIT ANALYSIS

The issue of global warming is an extremely difficult test for any decision-making methodology or policy-making process. Nevertheless, there are economists who bravely assert that cost–benefit analysis (CBA) can help. The British Treasury used cost–benefit analysis to justify the view that greenhouse gas emissions should be brought back down to 1990 levels by 2005 rather than 2000. Professor Nordhaus of Yale University has applied CBA to global warming, and come up with a series of recommendations as a result.

This appendix focuses in particular on Professor Nordhaus's views. It starts by summarising his argument and then looks at the problems involved, starting with the empirical problems about getting the right figures to put into the analysis and then considering the more basic issues about the logic and assumptions of the whole approach.

THE BEST ANALYSIS?

According to an editorial in *The Economist*, Professor William Nordhaus has produced 'The best (though magnificently simplified) cost–benefit analysis' of policies to combat global warming. It refers to 'Mr Nordhaus's hard-nosed calculations'.[1] Introducing an article by Nordhaus in which he summarises his views on the subject, *The Economist* said: 'Careful cost–benefit analysis, not panicky eco-action, is the right answer to the risk of global warming, says William D. Nordhaus ...'.[2] Nordhaus is a Professor of Economics at Yale University, and a former member of President Carter's Council of Economic Advisers. But just how 'hard-nosed' and 'careful' are his calculations?

Nordhaus set out his analysis in *To Slow or Not to Slow: The Economics of the Greenhouse Effect* (February 1990).[3] According to

Nordhaus, 'the subject is too important to be decided without using techniques that allow the balancing of costs and benefits in choosing the appropriate course of action'.[4]

On the costs side, he looks at various types of policies which have been proposed to slow down or prevent the greenhouse effect, and at the results which have been arrived at by studies of the effectiveness and costs of these different types of policies. He then produces estimates for the cost of bringing about different percentage reductions in greenhouse gases, using in each case the least expensive policies.

The costs of reducing greenhouse gas emissions are then compared with the benefits which would result. These benefits are the prevention of the damage which would otherwise be done by global warming. The benefits can therefore be quantified by quantifying the damage done by global warming at each possible level of greenhouse gas emissions. Estimates for this are arrived at primarily by considering the impact on different sectors of the US economy, thought to be severe for agriculture, moderate for construction and recreation, and negligible for manufacturing and most services.

The relative significance of the different sectors is assessed by using figures for their contribution to the total national income of the USA in 1981. The 'potentially severely impacted' sector of farms, forestry, and fisheries amounts to only about 3 per cent of national income, whereas there is only a negligible effect on 87 per cent of output.

Since even the 'severely impacted' agricultural sector will be far from being totally wiped out, the figure estimated for damage done is much less than the 3 per cent total for the sector. Nordhaus estimates that a doubling of carbon dioxide concentrations in the atmosphere would result in total damage to the US economy costed at just 0.28 per cent of Gross National Product (GNP).

The biggest leap in the argument is where Nordhaus says 'we will make the simplifying assumption that the damage applies to world GNP in 2050, and that the composition of world GNP is the same as U.S. GNP in 1981'.[5] This is presumably based on the view that economic development over seventy years will bring the economic structure of the world as a whole 'up to the level of' the USA now. In the paper's 'Conclusions', he says: 'This study has focussed primarily upon data based on the United States and extrapolated to the rest of the world.'[6]

Accepting that there are additional 'unmeasured and unmeasurable impacts', he increases his 'medium damage' figure of 0.28 per cent to 1

71

per cent of world total GNP. This represents the benefit which would be produced by preventing carbon dioxide concentrations (or their equivalent in other greenhouse gases) from doubling. Using data linking concentrations with emissions, Nordhaus then calculates what this amounts to in dollars per tonne of carbon dioxide (or its equivalent in other greenhouse gases).

These figures are then compared with figures for the cost of policies to achieve reductions in emissions, again expressing these in dollars per tonne. Comparing costs with benefits, Nordhaus finds that the 'most efficient level of control' of emissions is at 17 per cent below the level there would be with no government intervention to control emissions, because that is the level which gives the greatest excess of benefits over costs. Controlling emissions by more than that raises the costs more quickly than it raises the benefits, and eventually, at about the 26 per cent level, the costs become greater than the benefits. The conclusion is that governments should do something to prevent global warming, but be careful not to do too much.

GETTING THE FIGURES RIGHT

What are we to make of this analysis? There are many problems about it, some of which Nordhaus draws attention to in his paper. There are essentially two sorts of problems: problems about getting the right figures to put in the calculations (assuming that the argument itself is sound), and problems about the argument and approach itself. I shall consider first the problems about getting the right figures. There are four areas here which are problematic.

Firstly, there is uncertainty about what the environmental impact of increased emissions of greenhouse gases will actually be. Estimates have been produced for average global temperature increase, but it is far more difficult to predict regional and local impacts on rainfall, coastlines, and vegetation.

Secondly, even if we knew for certain what all the environmental impacts were going to be, it would be hard to predict the social and economic consequences of each of those impacts. Will changes in environmental conditions lead to large-scale migration? Will that migration lead to social conflict and war? Will the world's farmers respond to changes in climate in a way which shifts successfully from forms of agriculture appropriate to existing climates over to forms of agriculture appropriate to the new climatic conditions? How easily can societies and economies adapt to climatic and environmental change?

In order to produce a 'proper' cost–benefit analysis, we first need to know what the impacts will be, and then we can try to quantify them. In the case of global warming there is a lack of agreement about the likely environmental, economic, and social impacts themselves, and so there is also bound to be disagreement about the costs of those impacts. CBA cannot resolve this problem, it merely reflects it, or perhaps amplifies it. Nordhaus's policy conclusions, for example, do not derive primarily from his use of cost–benefit analysis to arrive at them. They depend mainly on his optimism about the likely effects of global warming, particularly on agriculture.

Thirdly, even if we knew for certain what the economic and social effects were going to be, it would still be difficult to quantify them in money terms. We need to know the severity of the effects in each sector, and the relative significance to attach to each sector. Nordhaus uses various existing studies of the likely severity of impacts, including a 1988 report by the US Environmental Protection Agency, and then quantifies their significance on the basis of national accounts statistics, which show the contribution of each sector of the economy to the GNP.

Fourthly, even if we knew for certain the economic costs of the effects of global warming, we would then need to compare them with the economic costs of the policies necessary to do something about it. There is clearly a great deal of uncertainty about the degree of effectiveness of different types of policies. A lot depends on the response of people to changes in prices and legislation. For example, how many car-drivers would switch to public transport if it became cheaper and petrol became more expensive? Figures for past elasticity of demand are used as though they were predictions about the future, but in a situation where so many variables are changing so rapidly they may not prove very reliable. Responses to changes in legislation and institutions are more difficult to predict than responses to changes in prices.

Part of the problem in calculating the net costs of policies is calculating benefits from those policies other than the benefits associated with reducing global warming. For example, a Norwegian study of the effects of doubling the price of fuel oil in 2010 showed large benefits would be derived from improvements in health due to a reduction in air pollution and from reductions in traffic accidents, noise, and congestion.[7] Policies to cope with the greenhouse effect through protecting rainforests would also contribute to maintaining biodiversity, and policies to control emissions of CFCs would help to conserve the ozone layer. There would also be benefits from spending the money raised if greenhouse gas emissions were controlled through taxation.

The empirical problems of arriving at reliable figures to put in cost–benefit calculations of policies to reduce global warming are therefore immense. These are not, however, my main concern here. It is conceivable that the empirical problems could be solved. It is always possible simply to go ahead on the basis of whatever appear to be the best estimates currently available. There are, however, a series of other problems about applying CBA to global warming, and each of these raise more fundamental difficulties.

PROBLEMS ABOUT USING GNP

Nordhaus bases his estimate for the economic cost of damage done by the greenhouse effect on national accounts statistics, looking at what each sector of the US economy contributes to US GNP. Nordhaus accepts that there are limitations in this approach. Writing in *The Economist*, he said:

> Many valuable goods and services escape the net of national-income accounting. Among the areas of importance are human health, biological diversity, amenity values of everyday life and leisure, and environmental quality. No one has done the sums here, so it is impossible to say whether the cost of climate change will be large or small.[8]

This is a rather large gap in the analysis!

There are really two separate parts of this problem. One is that there are many 'flows of welfare' where money doesn't change hands, which are therefore excluded from the GNP statistics. Global warming is likely to have an impact on some of these, such as the quality of leisure time. The second part of the problem is that global warming damages not only current flows of welfare and output, with the cost being measured as a loss in total output per year, it also damages the results of past output and existing stocks of natural resources and environmental capacity. Both of these categories excluded from the GNP accounts should be considered in any analysis of the costs of global warming.[9]

A further problem in this area concerns the position of other species. Non-human species only turn up in human national accounts when they are of economic value to human beings. For example, farm animals and many domestic pets are bought and sold in the market, and hence have particular money values. Cost–benefit analysis can go beyond the limits of the national accounts themselves by asking hypothetical questions about how much people would be prepared to pay if various other types of animals were bought and sold. What cost–benefit analysis does not do, however, is ask the animals. Presumably they want to go on living – and, with the exception of lemmings, their behaviour confirms this – but this wish is not turned into 'effective demand' because they have no money. They are only assigned a value in the analysis if human beings give them one.

This introduces a *bias against other species*, not just in the weak sense that human beings are seen as more valuable than members of other species (a view which I would want to defend), but also in the strong sense – much harder to justify – that non-human species are seen as having no intrinsic value in their own right, being dependent on humans to confer value upon them if we so choose. It is not just as a matter of degree that human beings are seen as more valuable, but two separate realms are imagined, and only one of these realms can assign value, with the other realm valueless unless human beings bestow value upon it.

Rapid habitat changes, and the extinctions which will result from a failure to adapt or migrate quickly enough, will only show up in cost–benefit analysis to the extent that they affect human beings. Since global warming will have a vast impact on non-human species this does not seem like a fair way of approaching the issue.

There is also a *bias against poorer countries* implicit in using GNP statistics as the basis of cost–benefit analysis. Bangladesh had a GNP of 18.3 billion US dollars in 1988.[10] Because much of Bangladesh is not far above sea-level, it is likely to be greatly affected by global warming. The GNP of the USA in 1988 was 4,863 billion US dollars.[11] It will also be affected by global warming, though not to so great an extent as Bangladesh.

If we put money values on the damage done by global warming based on GNP statistics, then it can be seen that even if the whole of Bangladesh were to be wiped out, that would count for less in the cost–benefit calculations than something like the loss of the US alcoholic drinks industry.

In his *Economist* article, Nordhaus says: 'the impacts of climate change on developed countries are likely to be small, probably amounting to less than 1% of national income over the next half-century. In contrast, small and poor countries with large agricultural sectors are particularly vulnerable.'[12]

Yet a cost–benefit analysis based around market money values will understate the impact of global warming on poor countries, whilst at the same time overstating the relative significance of the cost of richer countries implementing policies to control their greenhouse gas emissions. This can be illustrated by a hypothetical example, in which Country A is a rich country not much affected by global warming and Country B is a poor country greatly affected. Assume both would have to pay 3 per cent of GNP to bring about a substantial reduction in their emissions of greenhouse gases, sufficient to prevent global warming if adopted by all countries.

| | *Billions of dollars:* | |
	Country A	*Country B*
GNP	5,000	20
Cost of preventing warming	150	0.6
Cost of warming	50	2
	(1% of GNP)	(10% of GNP)

On these figures, Country A would suffer a net loss of 100 billion dollars by implementing policies to prevent global warming (i.e. 150 for the policies minus 50 saved by preventing warming). Country B would have a net gain of 1.4 billion dollars (2 saved by preventing warming, less 0.6 for the cost of the policies). Country A therefore finds it 'economically efficient' not to prevent global warming, whilst Country B finds it 'economically efficient' to prevent it.

But no country can prevent global warming by itself, because it is a global phenomenon. Suppose an international conference is called in this 'world' of two countries. Delegates from Country A and Country B agree to abide by the results of cost–benefit analysis. What happens?

Total costs of preventing warming are 150.6 billion dollars. Total benefits from preventing warming are 52 billion dollars. Therefore, net loss from preventing warming is 98.6 billion dollars. The conference therefore decides to let global warming go ahead. The use of GNP figures has biased the outcome in favour of the interests of Country A, even though it is less affected by the problem.

If we rerun the calculations on the basis of equal GNPs, keeping the same world total and the same proportions of GNP for the costs and benefits of preventing warming, we get:

| | Billions of dollars: | |
	Country A	Country B
GNP	2,510	2,510
Cost of preventing warming	75.3	75.3
Cost of warming	25.1	251

Country A still loses by preventing warming, Country B still gains. But this time the world totals are: Cost 150.6 Benefit 276.1. On the basis of equal GNPs, the cost–benefit analysis comes out in favour of implementing policies to prevent global warming.

Unless a deliberate adjustment is introduced to compensate for inequality in the distribution of income – in this case, in the distribution between different countries – cost–benefit analysis is bound to be biased against the interests of the poor. This is particularly important in the case of issues such as global warming, because much of the international debate about the subject revolves around conflicts of interest between rich and poor countries. Cost–benefit analysis is not a neutral way of resolving such conflicts.

THE FUTURE AND SUSTAINABILITY

According to Professor Nordhaus, 'the nature of the problem intrinsically involves incurring present costs to reduce potential future damages'.[13] It might seem at first sight that the obvious approach to such a problem is to add up the costs of a policy, add up the future damage which would be prevented, and compare the two. For example, suppose a policy costs 150 billion dollars, and brings a 20 billion dollar return each year for 12 years. The cost of 150 billion is apparently outweighed by the total benefit of 240 billion.

But cost–benefit analysis uses discount rates, which mean that a dollar next year is not worth as much as a dollar this year, and a dollar in 12 years' time is worth even less. With a discount rate of 10 per cent per year, the 20 billion dollar return in Year 2 is only worth 18 billion dollars, in Year 3 16.2 billion, in Year 4 14.6 billion, and so on.

Add all these up and the returns of 240 billion turn out to be worth only 143.5 billion – which is less than the cost of the policy.

The discount rate has changed the outcome of the analysis and introduced a *bias against the future*, and hence against future generations, understating the significance of the costs and benefits which apply to them relative to the significance of the costs and benefits which apply in the short-term. This has great practical significance for cost–benefit analysis of global warming, because although policies to restrain it may be expensive the benefits from such policies stretch far into the future. High discount rates mean that those future benefits won't count for very much.

If, however, we suppose that this bias against the future is removed in some way, so that equal costs and benefits are regarded equally at all points in time, problems about conflicts of interest between present and future generations still do not disappear. This is because it is perfectly possible that the costs (to present generations) of preventing warming may be greater than the benefits (to future generations) of preventing warming. If the costs are greater than the benefits, even a 'time-neutral' CBA will come out against bearing the costs.

This is contrary to the principle of 'sustainability'. The Brundtland Report defined this as meeting 'the needs of the present without compromising the ability of future generations to meet their own needs'.[14] This has been interpreted as entailing 'constant natural capital'. 'Conserving nature's capital is an instrumental rule for being fair to future generations.'[15] But cost–benefit analysis favours 'compromising the ability of future generations to meet their own needs' by running down 'nature's capital' whenever the costs of doing so are less than the benefits.

This can be illustrated by the case of Country C. In Country C, cost–benefit analysis has a great influence and the forests are always chopped down whenever the benefits from doing so are greater than the costs. Generation 1 starts with 1 million square miles of forest and chops down 10 per cent. Generation 2 chops down a further 10 per cent of the original area, and so on, until Generation 10, which chops down the remaining 100,000 square miles of forest. Generation 11 is left with no forest. Overall, the benefits turn out to have exceeded the costs, but even so, Generation 11 has lost out, 'constant natural capital' has not been maintained, and the needs of the first ten generations have been met at the expense of Generation 11. The use of cost–benefit analysis has not led to a policy of sustainability, nor is there any reason why it should be expected to. Cost–benefit analysis is concerned with totals (net costs or net benefits), whilst 'sustainability' is concerned with equity in distribution over time. They are quite different principles.

CONCLUSIONS

The application of cost–benefit analysis to global warming brings with it four main difficulties:

1 Empirical problems about getting correct figures for the impacts of global warming and for the degree of effectiveness of policies to combat it.
2 A bias against other species.
3 A bias against poorer countries.
4 A bias against future generations.

Far from being a way of impartially resolving either the empirical problems or the conflicts of interest involved in the issue, all of these problems and conflicts are reflected within the cost–benefit analysis itself. Not only that, but cost–benefit analysis implicitly takes sides, unless it is deliberately modified and adjusted in various ways, against the interests of those who most need to be protected and supported when global environmental issues are being considered.

Appendix 2

THE NEW ECONOMICS FOUNDATION

This book is one of a series, applying the New Economics to a variety of issues and areas of debate. It is the result of research carried out under the auspices of an organisation, the New Economics Foundation (NEF). This appendix is the text of a leaflet outlining what NEF is, and invites you to join us (see page 93 for details of how to become a supporter).

Environmental degradation, spreading deserts, unemployment and starvation, growing divisions between rich and poor, developed and 'undeveloped' – the economic system sometimes seems to be stacked against the world. It doesn't have to be like that. A growing number of people are working out new ideas, based on the work of New Economics pioneers like E. F. Schumacher, and linked with practical schemes that put people and planet first.

The emerging New Economics is humane, just, sustainable and based on people's needs. *New Economics* magazine – free to New Economics Foundation (NEF) supporters four times a year – charts its progress, reports on examples and spreads the ideas.

If you are active in one of the many movements that need a New Economics, whether your concern is environment, development or human rights, supporting NEF will keep you up to date with the latest developments and with the leading thinkers and doers in the field worldwide. You will also be backing the urgent search for an alternative to unrestrained growth and for badly needed solutions to humanity's most intractable problems – underpinning the work of environmental groups and development campaigns everywhere.

If you are simply interested in the way the world is changing, supporting NEF will put you at the fascinating and challenging frontiers of change.

NEF grew out of *The Other Economic Summit (TOES)*, founded in 1984 and now held every year in parallel to the seven richest nations' economic summit. Current projects and initiatives include:

- Developing work on alternative economic indicators.
- Spreading economic alternatives for Eastern and Central Europe.
- Researching links between economics, trade and the environment.
- Linking faith and ethics to economics.
- Understanding social investment and sustainable development.
- Promoting public debate on the problems of economic and financial integration in Western Europe.

We rely on the support of individuals and groups to carry on this important work, spreading understanding of New Economics ideas – showing people that there *are* solutions to today's awesome problems: human-scale solutions to which we can all contribute.

Appendix 3

BIBLIOGRAPHY

Books written by New Economics Foundation supporters include:

V. Anderson, *Alternative Economic Indicators*, London, Routledge, 1991.
J. Davis, *Greening Business*, Oxford, Basil Blackwell, 1991.
P. Ekins (with M. Hillman and R. Hutchison), *Wealth Beyond Measure*, London, Gaia Books, 1992.
P. Ekins, *A New World Order*, London, Routledge, 1992.
P. Ekins (ed.), *The Living Economy*, London, Routledge & Kegan Paul, 1986.
J. Robertson, *Future Wealth*, London, Cassell, 1989.

Similar approaches are evident in:

H. Daly and J. Cobb, *For the Common Good*, London, Green Print, 1990.
M. Jacobs, *The Green Economy*, London, Pluto Press, 1991.
D. Kemball-Cook, M. Baker, and C. Mattingly (eds), *The Green Budget*, London, Green Print, 1991.
M. A. Lutz and K. Lux, *Humanistic Economics*, New York, Bootstrap Press, 1988.
E. F. Schumacher, *Small is Beautiful*, London, Sphere, 1974.

For information about the greenhouse effect and energy efficiency, see the notes to specific chapters. Especially recommended is:

M. Grubb, *Energy Policies and the Greenhouse Effect*, Aldershot, Dartmouth Publishing Company:
Volume 1: *Policy Appraisal*, 1990.
Volume 2 (with P. Brackley, M. Ledic, A. Mathur, S. Rayner, J. Russell, A. Tanabe): *Country Studies and Technical Options*, 1991.

NOTES

INTRODUCTION

1 Mainstream environmental economics has also challenged the conception that using the atmosphere is costless, though from a less radical standpoint. See Appendix 1 for a critique of the application of cost-benefit analysis to the issue of global warming.

2 The OECD (Organisation for Economic Co-operation and Development) countries are: Canada, the United States of America, Japan, Australia, New Zealand, Austria, Belgium, Denmark, Finland, France, Germany, Greece, Iceland, Ireland, Italy, Luxembourg, The Netherlands, Norway, Portugal, Spain, Sweden, Switzerland, Turkey, the United Kingdom, and Yugoslavia.

As well as representing a large and significant part of the world, the OECD makes sense as an area to use for purposes of analysing energy policy because its economies are relatively similar, being industrialised and market-based (with the partial exceptions of Turkey and Yugoslavia); and member countries' energy consumption patterns have much more in common with each other than with those elsewhere. OECD experience is clearly relevant to the task of formulating future policies for the UK.

1 THE CARBON CRISIS

1 See S. Boyle and J. Ardill, *The Greenhouse Effect*, London, Hodder & Stoughton, 1989; and John Gribbin, *Hothouse Earth*, London, Bantam Press, 1990.

2 J. T. Houghton, G. J. Jenkins, and J. J. Ephraums (eds), *Climate Change: The IPCC Scientific Assessment*, Cambridge, Cambridge University Press, 1990.

3 For more information on acid pollution, see J. McCormick, *Acid Earth*, London, Earthscan, 1989.

4 Boyle and Ardill, op. cit., p. 181.

5 For estimates based on different scenarios, see B. Keepin and G. Kats, *Greenhouse Warming: A Rationale For Nuclear Power?*, Snowmass, Colorado, Rocky Mountain Institute, 1989.

6 See V. Anderson, *Alternative Economic Indicators*, London, Routledge, 1991.

2 THE PRICE OF AIR

1 World Commission on Environment and Development, *Our Common Future*, Oxford, Oxford University Press, 1987, p. 8.
2 Ministry of Housing, Physical Planning and Environment, *Highlights of the Dutch National Environmental Policy Plan*, The Hague, 1989, p. 6.
3 *Netherlands Environmental Policy Plan - Plus: Summary*, Document from the Dutch Embassy, London, pp. 10–11.
4 P. Johnson, S. McKay, and S. Smith, *The Distributional Consequences of Environmental Taxes*, London, Institute for Fiscal Studies, 1990. For US data, see R. J. Kopp and D. E. DeWitt, 'Distributional consequences of a Carbon Tax', in *Resources*, Fall 1991, pp. 6–8.
5 Ibid., p. 9, Table 2.1.1.
6 M. Pearson and S. Smith, *Taxation and Environmental Policy: Some Initial Evidence*, London, Institute for Fiscal Studies, 1990, p. 12.
7 The results of some recent studies are summarised in S. Barrett, 'Global warming: economics of a Carbon Tax', in D. Pearce (ed.), *Blueprint 2*, London, Earthscan, 1991, pp. 38–9.
8 M. Grubb, *Energy Policies and the Greenhouse Effect*, vol. 1, Aldershot, Dartmouth, p. 95.
9 Attempts have been made to quantify this: see Appendix 1.

3 ARGUMENTS AND TRENDS

1 See M. Jacobs, *The Green Economy*, London, Pluto Press, 1991.
2 *OECD Environmental Data Compendium 1989*, Paris, Organisation for Economic Co-operation and Development, 1989, p. 227.
3 Ibid., p. 305.
4 Ibid., p. 229.
5 Calculated from data in ibid., p. 311.
6 Ibid., p. 227.
7 *Financial Times*, 19 October 1990.
8 'Summary of IPCC Working Group 1 conclusions', in M. Grubb, *Energy Policies and the Greenhouse Effect*, vol. 1, Aldershot, Dartmouth, p. 8.
9 See A. Agarwal and S. Narain, *Global Warming in an Unequal World*, New Delhi, Centre for Science and Environment, 1991; and F. Krause, W. Bach, and J. Koomey, *Energy Policy in the Greenhouse*, London, Earthscan Publications, 1990.
10 Calculated from figures given in World Resources Institute, *World Resources 1988/89*, Oxford, Oxford University Press, pp. 306–7; and OECD, op. cit., p. 305.
11 M. Grubb, 'What to do about global warming', *International Affairs*, vol. 66, no. 1 (January 1990), p. 84.
12 C. Flavin, 'Slowing global warming', in L. R. Brown *et al.*, *State of the World 1990*, New York, W. W. Norton, 1990, p. 19.

13 J. H. Gibbons, P. D. Blair, and H. L. Gwin, 'Strategies for energy use', *Scientific American*, September 1989, p. 91.
14 *Greenhouse Gas Emissions: The Energy Dimension*, Paris, Organisation for Economic Co-operation and Development/International Energy Agency, 1991, pp. 96–102.
15 A. P. Fickett, C. W. Gellings, A. B. Lovins, 'Efficient uses of electricity', *Scientific American*, September 1990, p. 31.

4 TWENTY REASONS FOR ENERGY INEFFICIENCY

1 A. F. Beijdorff, *Energy Efficiency*, London, Shell International Petroleum Company, 1979, p. 16.
2 M. Grubb, *Energy Policies and the Greenhouse Effect*, vol. 1, Aldershot, Dartmouth, p. 115.

5 POLICIES FOR ENERGY EFFICIENCY

1 International Energy Agency, *Energy Conservation in IEA Countries*, Paris, Organisation for Economic Co-operation and Development/International Energy Agency, 1987, pp. 124–31.
2 International Energy Agency, *Electricity End-Use Efficiency*, Paris, Organisation for Economic Co-operation and Development/International Energy Agency, 1989, p. 96.
3 Ibid., p. 105.
4 International Energy Agency, *Energy Conservation in IEA Countries*, op. cit., pp. 147–53.
5 See ibid., pp. 162–5.
6 Ibid., p. 171.
7 Ibid., pp. 136–45.

6 UK POLICIES

1 See M. Grubb, P. Brackley, M. Ledic, A. Mathur, S. Rayner, J. Russell, and A. Tanabe, *Energy Policies and the Greenhouse Effect*, vol. 2, Aldershot, Dartmouth Publishing Company, 1991, pp. 187–91.
2 Department of Energy, *Proof of Evidence for the Sizewell 'B' Public Inquiry*, London, Department of Energy, 1982, A3.
3 Committee of Public Accounts, *National Energy Efficiency*, London, House of Commons, 1990, p. vi, para. 6.
4 Conservative Research Department, *The Campaign Guide 1987*, London, Conservative and Unionist Central Office, 1987, pp. 184–5.
5 See J. Roberts, D. Elliott, and T. Houghton, *Privatising Electricity*, London, Belhaven Press, 1991, especially Chapter 7.
6 Quoted in *The Fifth Fuel*, London, Association for the Conservation of Energy, Spring 1989.

7 'Memorandum from the Association for the Conservation of Energy', in Committee of Public Accounts, op. cit., p. 15.
8 Friends of the Earth, *How Green is Britain?*, London, Hutchinson Radius, 1990, p. 42.
9 Committee of Public Accounts, op. cit., p. ix, para 16.
10 Ibid., p. xii, para. 36.
11 Department of the Environment, *This Common Inheritance*, London, 1990, p. 71, para. 5.35.
12 Ibid., p. 64, para. 5.1.
13 Ibid., p. 284, para. C.11.
14 Ibid., p. 286, para. C.22.
15 Ibid., p. 287, para. C.29.
16 Ibid., p. 69, para. 5.25–6.
17 *Financial Times*, 26 September 1990.
18 *Daily Telegraph*, 26 September 1990.
19 Department of the Environment, op. cit., p. 73, para 5.44.

7 LEAST COST PLANNING

1 Quoted in *Lessons From America No. 5*, London, Association for the Conservation of Energy, p. 24.
2 Quoted in *Lessons from America No. 4*, London, Association for the Conservation of Energy, p. 17.
3 International Energy Agency, *Electricity End-Use Efficiency*, Paris, Organisation for Economic Co-operation and Development/International Energy Agency, 1989, p. 145.
4 Ibid., p. 146.
5 *Regulating for Efficiency*, London, Association for the Conservation of Energy, p. 10.
6 International Energy Agency, op. cit., p. 145.
7 *Lessons from America No. 2*, London, Association for the Conservation of Energy, pp. 7–9.
8 *Electricity in IEA Countries: Issues & Outlook*, Paris, Organisation for Economic Co-operation and Development/International Energy Agency, 1985, p. 52.

8 POLICY CONCLUSIONS

1 See E. Brown, P. Conaty, and C. Kunz: *Fuelsavers: A Feasibility Study*, Birmingham, Community Energy Research, Birmingham Settlement Money Advice Services, and Birmingham Settlement Research Unit, 1990.

APPENDIX 1

1 *The Economist*, 27 October 1990.
2 *The Economist*, 7 July 1990.

3 W. Nordhaus, *To Slow or Not to Slow: The Economics of the Greenhouse Effect*, New Haven, Conn., Yale University, Department of Economics, mimeo., 1990.

4 Ibid., p. 2.

5 Ibid., p. 24.

6 Ibid., p. 32.

7 S. Glomsrod *et al.*, *Stabilization of Emissions of CO_2: A Computable General Equilibrium Assessment*, Oslo, Central Bureau of Statistics, 1990, quoted in D. Pearce (ed.), *Blueprint 2*, London, Earthscan, 1991, p. 21.

8 W. Nordhaus, in *The Economist*, 7 July 1990.

9 For more details of what is excluded from national income accounts, see V. Anderson, *Alternative Economic Indicators*, London, Routledge, 1991.

10 United Nations Development Programme, *Human Development Report 1991*, New York, Oxford University Press, 1991, p. 165.

11 Ibid., p. 192.

12 Nordhaus, in *The Economist*, 7 July 1990.

13 Nordhaus, *To Slow or Not to Slow*, op. cit., p 3.

14 World Commission on Environment and Development, *Our Common Future*, Oxford, Oxford University Press, 1987, p. 8.

15 D. Pearce, 'Economics and the global environmental challenge', *Millenium*, London, Millenium Publishing Group, London School of Economics, Winter 1990, vol. 19, no. 3, p. 366.

INDEX

I would like to become a NEF Supporter as:

[   ] A core supporter of NEF at £100 minimum a year.

[   ] A regular supporter at £15 minimum a year.

[   ] An unwaged supporter at £8 a year (reduced rate for unemployed people, students, pensioners, etc.).

[   ] I enclose a donation to support NEF's work.

[   ] Please send a banker's order and tax recovery form.

I enclose a cheque for £ .... made out to 'New Economics Foundation'. Please add £5 if your address is outside the UK.

Name ....

Address ....

....

Please send to New Economics Foundation, 88-94 Wentworth Street, London E1 7SA.